Ghosts Like Bacon

Samantha Red Wolf

Copyright © 2018 Samantha Red Wolf

All rights reserved. No part of this publication may be reproduced, distributed, or transmitted in any form or by any means, including photocopying, recording, or other electronic or mechanical methods, without the prior written permission of the publisher, except in the case of brief quotations embodied in critical reviews and certain other noncommercial uses permitted by copyright law.

ISBN: 9781983035449

—TABLE OF CONTENTS—

Chapter 1: Beyond the Veil	1
Chapter 2: The Black Cloud	6
Chapter 3: Ghost Dog	11
Chapter 4: The Obnoxious Ghost	19
Chapter 5: The Warm Lady	28
Chapter 6: Protection from Negative Spirits	34
Chapter 7: The Boy and the Box	47
Chapter 8: The Travelling Penny	57
Chapter 9: Luna and the Tuna	61
Chapter 10: The Man in the Bowler Hat	71
Chapter 11: The Corpse in the Closet	77
Chapter 12: The House of Light	80
Chapter 13: The Moldy Man	85

Chapter 14: The Feather	90
Chapter 15: The Earthquake	94
Chapter 16: The Guardian Spirit	100
Chapter 17: The Ghost Snake	105
Chapter 18: The Cheerful Soldier	110
Chapter 19: Alice's Tears	116
Chapter 20: Ghosts Like Puppies Too	125
Chapter 21: Energy Cords	130
Chapter 22: Ghost Mouse	135
Chapter 23: Hitchhiking Ghosts	138
Chapter 24: How *Ghosts Like Bacon* Got Its Name and Other Stories	142
Chapter 25: Out of the Darkness	146
Chapter 26: Ghostly Conclusions	151
About the Author	159

—CHAPTER 1—
BEYOND THE VEIL

There aren't many people who understand what my daughter and I go through daily. Some might think we're a little crazy – a couple French fries short of a happy meal. But I can assure you, if you've stumbled onto this book and are curious enough to read it, everything in these pages happened exactly as it was written. There is no need for a made-up story, since my life is stranger than fiction.

My daughter, whom I will call "Kiani", was born with the ability to see the spirit world. I'm not exactly sure why or how, but I do know she's not the only one.

I once watched a video online in which a man explained how to see energy in the air. He said if you're relaxed and do it right, the air around you takes on a "staticky look", like pixels over a TV screen.

When I told my daughter this, she was surprised. "But...that's normal for me. *Everywhere* is static. The world doesn't look like that to you?"

"Nope," I replied. "Crystal-clear."

It's my opinion that she has been this way since she was a baby, though I don't know for sure.

She was always vocal; full of laughter and chatter but quiet in public. Most of the time, she would just quietly glance at strangers, like many shy kids do. But when she was baby, she would sometimes look at someone and completely flip out. She'd burst into frightened tears, turn away from them and then attempt, quite impossibly, to hide behind me by crawling up over my shoulder. It was more than a little awkward. I would always say something like, "I'm sorry. She's shy with people she doesn't know."

I thought it was odd behavior at the time, but now, I often wonder what it was she saw when she looked at these strangers. Were they accompanied by some malevolent entity that only my daughter could see? I guess I'll never know because she doesn't remember it.

As she got a little older, she became frightened of "monsters" in her room. It's common for kids her age, so I thought nothing of it. She often talked of red-eyed creatures looking in through her windows and dark shapes outside on the street, and I would soothe her with phrases like, "It's all right, honey. You're just tired, and things around you can look a little weird when the lights are off."

Her fear of sleeping alone was so bad that I never bothered to enforce it much. She had her own room when she was four, but it served more as a toy room than anything. I never used cribs when the kids were babies either, opting instead for two gigantic, Japanese-style mattresses laid back-to-back so that we could all sleep in the same room, if we wanted to. No falling out of bed, no baby monitors, no staggering from my bedroom at two a.m. to the call of a crying child, etc.

When she was five, things got a little more intense. Once, she came to me crying because she saw a torso of a man (no arms, legs, or head) hovering upright over the stairs. Then, around the same time, both my kids were frightened because a plastic playset next to them had lifted a few inches off the floor and crashed back down.

The little stories continued, and I kept casual about them. I listened and nodded and tried not to react much one way or another, partly because I didn't want to inspire fear before I understood what was going on.

I wasn't exactly inexperienced with occurrences of the paranormal variety, and if this wasn't just childish imagination, then I knew instinctively that fear could often amplify activity such as this. You see, I have "intuitive gifts" of my own, which seem to run in the family. I'd had experiences with both good and bad spirits, but they were rare, and I didn't know what to think of what she told me at the time. If they were bad spirits, then ignoring them was the best option (don't give them power by paying them attention), followed by prayer and use of The Great Spirit's name, if that failed.

I was raised Christian but became simply "spiritual" in my twenties. Later, due partly to my Native American genes, I ditched Christianity altogether and considered myself to be mostly Native American Spiritual. I believed in a Creator (The Great Spirit) and good and bad spirits, of course, but I was still undecided on ghosts. Though Native American tribes believe(d) that the spirits of our ancestors can hear and respond to us, I'd never experienced a "human spirit" personally. Did they exist? I had no idea.

—CHAPTER 2—
THE BLACK CLOUD

The time of dismissing my daughter's gifts as childish imagination was about to be a thing of the past. What I experienced next was a step toward acceptance.

My daughter was ten years old then. It had been a rough few months for me. I had been in an emotional battle with someone close to me, and I knew I had to get away from them. I knew the term "energy vampire", and this one was far worse than any I'd ever encountered.

One day, I went upstairs and laid down for a much-needed nap. Though I'd hoped for a peaceful sleep, it was far from it. I had the most terrible, violent, hate-filled nightmare. I don't recall the details, but I do recall the terror it filled me with. During it, I became aware that I was dreaming and forced my eyes open.

There, hovering directly above my face, was what I can only describe as a black, smoky cloud. My eyes widened at the sight, and the cloud screamed at me. It was a sound of pure anger and disappointed frustration. Then the cloud spread out and faded into nothing, like smoke from a cigar.

It freaked me out. I can't deny it. My empath ability (sensing and feeling emotions from others) made it worse because I had felt its emotion and intention. Whatever it was, it had been feeding off my suffering, like a leech sucking blood, and my coming awake broke its hold on me.

I didn't sleep well at all that night.

Shortly after this incident, a few days after dumping the energy vampire, my daughter came to me with tear-filled eyes.

"Mommy, I have to talk to you."

I was immediately concerned.

"What is it? Are you okay?"

"I need to tell you something."

"What's wrong? Did someone hurt you?"

"No," she said, fresh tears filling her eyes. "I just don't want you to be upset or think I'm weird."

"Baby, what? I won't be upset. What's

happened? Are you sure no one's hurt you?"

"No, no one's hurt me."

"You can tell me anything," I told her. "I won't be mad at you or think you're weird. Besides, you're already weird anyway," I added.

She laughed a little and wiped at her eyes. "Remember all the scary monsters I see?"

"Yeah."

"Well, it's much worse than that. I see *all kinds* of stuff. Every single day..."

She went on in more detail, and I listened quietly, only stopping to ask questions to clarify her descriptions.

It wasn't just shadows on the sidewalk or eyes outside her windows. It was people that look like regular people who vanish into thin air while you look at them. It was humans lacking any color at all, like actors in black-and-white films, but always missing random body parts – an arm here, both legs, half of a face. It was human-shaped shadow figures, walking around corners and into walls. It was pure white forms, fragile and crooked, like badly formed people made of paper mâché. There were also animals. Cats and dogs, deer that stood in misty forms at the edges of forests, and even, much to my surprise, lizard-like humanoids, roaming the halls of her elementary school.

Now, as shocking as this all was, I felt her sincerity and knew she was telling the truth. I also knew how hard I had worked to raise my kids to be honest people. "You are only as good as your word," my Grandfather used to say, and I had made this a motto in my house over the years.

"I believe you," I told her. "But listen carefully. I want us to make a promise to each other." I stopped and looked at her, emphasizing how serious I was.

"Okay," she said.

"If you promise to *always* tell me the truth about what you see, with no exaggerating, then I promise to *always* believe you. Deal?"

She nodded happily. "I promise," she said.

Then her eyes got sad again.

"Mommy. I'm scared. I don't want to be scared. I try not to be, but...there's this little girl...she's been following me around the house all day. She's black-and-white, like an old TV show, and her arm and part of her face are missing. Her eyes are all dark, with circles under them, and she looks at me like she wants something. She scares me."

I don't recall everything I told her after this, but

I do remember telling her that she had to understand that along with all these scary spirits she sees, there are, without a doubt, *good and protective* spirits too. I had encountered these gentle beings a few times over the years, and many members of the family had as well. The stories were so plentiful combined that you could almost fill a book with them.

I told her that she was a child of The Great Spirit and that he, along with her Guardian Spirit, have always and will always protect her. I told her that I would pray on it and think on it, and together, we would help her overcome her fear.

"The biggest and the greatest of all the spirits is The Great Spirit, and *you are his child,*" I told her. "Whatever you see every day...they are little fish in The Great Spirit's pond. There is no bigger fish than him. Stick by his side and nothing can touch you."

And we live by this truth every day.

After our conversation, I delved into research on children with her abilities. What I discovered helped not only her but me as well.

—CHAPTER 3—
GHOST DOG

Everything changed once the secret was out. Ghosts were a reality I could no longer ignore, thanks to my daughter's decision to tell me everything.

I knew instinctively that her gifts weren't something I could just wish away. They were a reality to her, and even though I couldn't see them, like she could, I felt determined to protect her from the bad ones.

I dove into researching how I could help her and soon discovered something that would change everything drastically for us.

Both were herbs, and the first was periwinkle.

Known in medieval times as "the sorcerer's violet", this little plant was believed to have medicinal properties and possess the ability to ward off evil spirits. It was said to be especially beneficial for the protection of children.

I found a little shop online that sold periwinkle amulets and immediately purchased a couple for Kiani and myself. They came in a little vial on a cord, and I gave one to her, instructing her to wear it constantly, outside showers and baths.

I also bought a bundle of sage and began smudging the house daily, saying a prayer of blessing as I went.

The effect was immediate.

After a few days of seeing nothing out of the ordinary, my daughter came to me and said it was working. She said she didn't even see spirits outside of the house, at her friend's houses, or at her dad's, when she visited.

I was thrilled! And not only for her but myself as well. I had suffered from terrible, violent nightmares since I was a child, and they suddenly stopped. I had almost forgotten what a great night's sleep was!

A couple weeks later, I had an experience, which I should mention before continuing.

I was at my acupuncturist's office, being treated for allergies. It was quiet and peaceful. She had loaded me up with a few carefully placed needles and then left the room, closing the door behind her so that I could rest.

I used this time to go into a semi-meditative state. I wasn't a fan of full meditation. The one time I had tried it, it had scared me near to death because my spirit had almost left my body. I remember a suffocating, panicky feeling, as if I were about to die. Then, when I opened my eyes to look down at my feet, all I saw was the wall to the right of my feet. My real feet were left of me because my spirit had shifted right, leaving only my head where it should be. I panicked and snapped back in. Not my thing.

As I lay there then, in my much safer headspace, lazily watching the colors shift and change behind my eyelids, I heard a distant sound from the reception room and pulled up out of it a bit. Except I knew I wasn't alone.

In "my mind's eye", I "saw" a wolf laying on the floor by me. Its head was turned in the direction of the sound I had heard, ears perked forward. It listened for a moment, then relaxed, turned its head forward, and began panting gently, much in the casual way a pet dog would, while waiting on its favorite human.

Instantly, I heard two words in my head.

Guardian.

And a word that wasn't English.

Feyla.

I knew in my gut that this was my Guardian Spirit.

I mention this because my wolf played a part in what happened a few weeks later, when Kiani began seeing spirits again. Because oh, did she ever! Only this time, what my daughter saw and felt was quite different.

First, she started seeing spirits in snatches in the distance and then up closer. They were not the tortured, scary beings she was used to seeing quite commonly. They were harmless old ladies, smiling gentlemen in old hats, and dogs and cats by the dozens.

They came through our house all times of the day, even after saging. We quickly concluded that sage and periwinkle had no effect on gentle spirits. In fact, one little animal spirit seemed to prefer showing up right after we saged, as if he were hiding out, waiting for us to clean the area of "bad stuff" first.

We later surmised that perhaps negative spirits made gentle spirits uncomfortable and less likely to enter a house filled with them. I can't say I blame them.

One day, Kiani came to me and said, "Mommy! There is a little animal following me around, and I can only see it in flashes. All I know is that it is cream-colored. When I look directly at it, it vanishes. But I can feel its energy."

She got down on the ground and felt the air over a space above the floor no taller than ten inches.

"If you put your hands here, you can feel it. It's all buzzy-feeling. Try it!"

I shrugged and knelt to feel the same patch of air.

"I don't feel anything," I said.

She looked disappointed for a moment, then went back to interacting with the little animal, trying out different positioning of her hands, walking away, and then following her senses back to it.

I smiled to myself over the thought of how funny this would look to someone who didn't understand what was going on.

I headed upstairs to put away the laundry.

A couple minutes later, Kiani came into the room.

"Mommy, this is driving me crazy! I don't know what this is! It's either a cat or a dog, but I can't see it!"

I glanced at her and grabbed a hanger in one hand and a shirt in the other.

"I don't know, sweetie. Maybe just keep trying."

She walked toward me. "I bet you could help me. What if you asked your wolf to tell us?"

"What do you mean?" I asked, curious. I hung the shirt up and reached for another hanger.

"I mean, close your eyes and ask the wolf."

I blinked at her. "Uh...I suppose I could try that...can't hurt."

She nodded happily at me. I put the hanger back and followed her into the bedroom.

I laid down on the floor and gave it my best shot. I closed my eyes and said the wolf's name (Feyla), then asked it to help us know what kind of animal Kiani was seeing.

I didn't have to wait long.

Dog.

The word jumped into my head with a little thump, like a frog onto a lily pad.

I repeated it to Kiani.

"Thank you!" she exclaimed. Then, "Come here, doggie. Come here!"

I sat up and watched her wonderingly for a minute or so.

"You know what's weird?" she pondered.

"What?"

"I can't see him, but I can feel where he is and what he's doing. Isn't that strange?"

"Very," I replied.

"I do know what he looks like, though. He is cream-colored with brown spots on his ears, like he has mud on him."

Instantly, my mind recalled my neighbor from across the street. She once had a little dog, maybe five years ago. It had been run over after escaping the house on one of his many mischievous explorations.

But that couldn't be him. I remembered him being all white, with no brown spots.

What the heck?

Without telling Kiani was I was doing, I texted my neighbor and asked her what her dog's name had been because I couldn't recall.

She texted back: "Gino."

I said thanks and then, still in full Sherlock mode, I got on my neighbor's social media page and looked back through old photos until I found Gino.

I'll be damned.

Gino had been cream, with little patches of brown on his ears. So much for my memory of him.

I didn't tell Kiani.

Instead, I put my phone down and said, "Ki, I have an idea. Let's try and guess what the dog's name is!"

Her eyes lit up. "Yes!" she said. "Good idea!"

"How about I think up names, and you see if the dog responds to them?"

"Okay!"

I started listing off a variety of names. Spot, Tippy, Ralph ("Mommy! That's a terrible name!), Harry, Fluffy, etc. Each time, Kiani would tell me the dog's response; he is just sitting there, he wagged his tail once, he is looking at the window.

Then...I slipped in Gino.

Immediately, Kiani said, "Mommy, stop! He just looked up at you, wagged his tail, and ran over to you! Do you think that's his name?"

I couldn't help but laugh. "Yep," I said. "I would say that's his name for sure."

—CHAPTER 4—
THE OBNOXIOUS GHOST

I had never seen a ghost of a human. It figures that when I finally did, it wouldn't be what I expected.

Nor did I expect that this would be *the strangest* day of my life.

The house the kids and I had been living in was too big for us, especially after my divorce a couple years back. Money was tight, and I knew I couldn't afford to keep it any longer.

Fortunately, my mother, whom I'm close to, lived just down the street and had a loft apartment upstairs, which she said we were welcome to use. Since I was already accustomed to driving up and down the street to help her with errands and chores (she has bad knees and can't walk well), it made a lot of sense to move in with her.

One day, toward the end of our move, I told Kiani to come with me to our old house and pick out the remaining toys she wanted to keep, leaving the rest in bags for charity. I told her that she could do that while I mowed the lawn.

When we got to the house, Kiani scampered upstairs with her plastic bags, and I headed out back with the lawnmower.

I was just finishing up the last stretch of grass when I saw a flash of a child in a red shirt run past the house to the left of me.

I slowed down and looked, expecting to see my daughter, but there was nothing there. Besides, I remembered her wearing a pink shirt.

Hmm. Weird.

I shrugged it off and finished up, then headed back into the house to check on Kiani. Her timing was perfect, as I walked up to see her hauling her two bags downstairs.

"All done!" she said. "I left the charity bags upstairs."

"Okay. I'll pick them up tomorrow," I replied.

I had just about forgotten what I had seen in the backyard. I loaded the bags into the car, and Kiani walked around to the passenger side.

I was climbing into the driver's seat when she stopped and stepped a few paces away from the car, peering in the direction of the backyard. Then she opened the passenger side door and climbed in.

"Mommy!" she whispered, "I just saw a boy in the backyard."

"Oh? What did he look like?"

"He had a red shirt on."

I stared at her in surprise for a few seconds.

"A red shirt?"

"Yep."

"That's weird," I said. "I thought I saw a kid in a red shirt run past me outside, but when I turned and looked, he wasn't there."

We put two and two together and figured that it must have been a spirit, which wasn't surprising...but *me* seeing it was.

As I pulled out of the driveway and headed back down the street to my mother's house, Kiani became increasingly alarmed.

"Mommy..."

"What?"

"Mommy, he's following us."

"He is?" I asked, wondering why she sounded so freaked out.

"I can feel his personality..."

I waited for her to say more, slowing down a bit and looking at her in glances.

"He is not a nice kid," she continued, "like, *at all*. He was obnoxious when he was alive, and he's obnoxious now."

"You feel like he's following us? Are you sure?"

"Yes! Mommy, we *do not* want him coming inside! We need to sage the house quickly, before Grandma gets back!"

I agreed.

My mother, whom I'd inherited my Native American genes from, was *far* from un-gifted. But unfortunately, with her being nearly eighty and mostly conservative Christian, we didn't dare to share our experiences with her. To my mother, there are only angels or demons. Nothing in-between. She would be terrified if she knew, and it would serve no point anyway. My mother is a content and happy lady.

We pulled into my mom's driveway and got out of the car. As Kiani walked around the back, I heard the distinct and unmistakable sound of a child humming.

I didn't have a chance to remark on it because

Kiani immediately said, "Humming. You hear it?"

"Yes."

(Later, it dawned on Kiani that the boy had been humming the same tune my daughter had been in her bedroom, while packing her toys.)

"Quick!" Kiani called, running for the door. "Sage, Mommy!"

"I'm on it!" I called back.

I left the bags in the car, went into the house and upstairs, to the sage bundle.

I quickly and thoroughly smudged every room, door, and window in the house, speaking firmly as I walked, asking The Great Spirit to protect and seal the house from unwelcome spirits.

When I finished, I looked at my daughter, who nodded and smiled.

She said the boy had stood outside the front door for a bit, then turned and left.

Relief.

We headed upstairs to rest and naturally assumed the drama was over, but something else unexpected happened.

See, the little ghost dog from the last story had gone missing for a couple weeks prior to this. Kiani was accustomed to seeing him a lot in our old house, but it had been long enough that she had occasionally voiced concern that Gino hadn't followed us over to the new house.

"He's afraid of going outside now," Kiani had said a while back. "I think it was because of how he died, being hit by a car. Every time someone opens the front or back door, he runs and gets up on the couch."

Kiani had been worried that he couldn't find his way to us.

Well, as we were resting upstairs, glad to be rid of the obnoxious ghost boy, Kiani suddenly sat up and gasped.

"Mommy! Gino's here!"

"Oh, good," I said. "I'm so glad. Maybe he followed us this time."

"No, he only just got here. He wasn't here when we got home – wait..."

Her eyes widened.

"There's another dog here! He's big and black, with brown tips on his mouth, ears, and legs. His ears are pointy."

It sounded like a Doberman Pinscher to me. I showed her a picture of one on my phone.

She said, "That's it!"

Kiani continued to explain what she saw. She felt that this dog had led Gino over to our house and that they were obviously friends. She was further amazed that the dog didn't leave right away. Instead, he stuck around for a while, lounging lazily beside Gino, who was obviously excited to be here. The Doberman panted and made casual, gentle swipes at the smaller dog with his much bigger paws.

Then Kiani further surprised me by announcing a *third* visitor.

"It's your wolf!" she said happily. "I know it."

(Later, it dawned on me that Feyla had shown up as a response to my prayers for protection. I'm guessing it did a quick patrol of the house before heading upstairs to check on us.)

I listened, fascinated, as she described the beautiful tones of the wolf's coat. She described it as being quite large; the top of its back was about the height of my waist.

I was completely in awe at this point. This had been one of the *strangest* days of my life, and all I wanted to do was just watch and listen, as Kiani did her best to explain what she saw with her amazing eyes.

"The black dog's name," Kiani said, "starts with an R."

For some reason — most likely because the wolf was there — the letters O, C, and K jumped into my head. I immediately said them out loud, pausing at K because I realized Kiani was saying the same letters simultaneously.

She kept going, "Y."

"Rocky," we both said, again in unison.

This is nuts, I thought to myself.

Then she described one of the sweetest things, and I'll never forget it.

Feyla laid down next to Rocky, and both watched Gino for a while. The little dog was overly excited. He kept bounding back and forth between the two larger animals and crouching down, with his butt up and tail wagging, in the universal doggie language of "Let's play!"

Rocky kept with the casual, gentle swipes at Gino, but Feyla did something quite unexpected. The wolf lowered its massive head, stretched it out, and nuzzled the little dog, much like a mother dog affectionately nuzzles her babies.

It seemed to calm Gino down, and soon after, Rocky and Feyla got up and left, leaving Gino with us. He stretched out on the bed we sat on, quite content to be back with his friend, a remarkable little girl with eyes *that could see him*.

—CHAPTER 5—
THE WARM LADY

Sometimes, a spirit is unable to move on because of guilt and worry over their remaining loved ones. Wandering amid a sea of people, some will notice something unusual, like a light in the distance. When they realize it's coming from a human, many feel drawn to approach this human.

One sweet, female spirit found herself drawn to my daughter's light and started spending a lot of time in our house.

For about six weeks, Kiani had seen a woman with shoulder-length, dark brown hair. She appeared in solid form, like a regular person, and mostly when my mother (who lives downstairs) was listening to gospel music and recorded sermons from some of her favorite pastors.

When Kiani went downstairs to talk to her

Grandma, she would see the woman standing nearby or walking to and from the room.

Once, Kiani heard the woman say in a warm, friendly voice, "Well, good morning to you!"

"I don't know who that lady is," Kiani said to me one day, "but she sure is nice!"

Now, as I mentioned in the last chapter, my mom doesn't know about Kiani's gifts, and we don't bother her with them. But I often wonder if it truly was my daughter's light or something about my mother that drew her. If it *was* Kiani, then the lady visitor found the most comfort in my mother's company.

One morning, my mom surprised me by asking if myself or the kids had come into her bedroom and bathroom around three a.m.

"No," I told her. "We were all asleep. We occasionally get up, but it's only to use our own bathrooms. No reason to come into yours."

"Hmm," she said. "That's so strange. I woke up because I heard my bedroom door open. Then I heard someone walk across the floor and into my bathroom. I thought it must be you or the kids, so I went back to sleep."

I told her that was, indeed, strange, and she

finally shrugged and said it must have been a dream.

It wasn't long after this that Kiani saw the lady upstairs, and I decided on a whim to try to contact her. We both felt that she needed help in some way.

I asked The Great Spirit and my Guardian Spirit, the wolf, to help me. Then I picked up my tarot deck. I had never tried using my deck to communicate with the spirit world before, other than with The Great Spirit directly, but it was worth a shot.

I called out to the lady, asking her to come closer. I told her that we meant her no harm and wanted to speak with her for a little while.

She didn't appear, but I felt her energy as she approached.

(This was a wonderous time for me. Thanks to my daughter, I was learning not just about *her* psychic gifts but a bit about my own as well. I began to pay attention to the energy around me and to my feelings of being watched, which I'd always just assumed was some weird paranoia of mine.)

"These are tarot cards," I told her. "I'm going to ask you some questions, and I hope that by using them, I'll be able to hear you in a way."

My empath ability and Kiani's strong energy made a great team.

I started laying out cards, some in general and some specific. The first feeling I got from her was that she didn't like my tarot cards. She felt they were bad and something I shouldn't be using. She felt hesitant to talk to me in this way, but she also wanted to be heard, so she stayed by me, cautious but listening.

Interesting, I thought.

Next, I asked her who she was. I pulled a card and words came to me.

Mother of four children.

I said this out loud and then asked her name. She didn't reply, but I kept getting the impression that she didn't want me to know her name. Then she gave me a name (*Tonya*), which confused me because I knew it wasn't hers.

I let it go. "Why do you hang out downstairs so much?"

Christian. Comforting.

So, she was Christian. She found comfort in my mom's activities.

"How did you die?"

Car accident.

I asked her why she was still here.

Worried about my kids.

Then...

Guilt.

I felt that her kids were alive and that they were mourning her terribly. Their suffering broke her heart. She blamed herself for the accident and the suffering it caused.

No wonder she wasn't moving on.

I followed my gut and told her I felt, without a doubt, that her family loves her. I said that car accidents happen even to the best of drivers and that it wasn't her fault. I told her that her family is sad, but they will be okay, and that God will watch over her family, so that she needn't worry about them.

Then I told her that when she was ready, all she had to do was follow my wolf and that my wolf would lead her to where she needs to go.

My daughter never saw her again after that.

But the next day, I found out something amazing.

On another whim, I checked the internet, looking for articles about a mother of four that had died in a car accident, close to our city, around the same time Kiani started seeing her.

There were only two, but one was a blonde lady and didn't fit the time close enough.

The other one lead to an article and an obituary. The woman in the photos had lived in a town only a half-hour from us. She had dark brown, shoulder-length hair and had died a few days before Kiani first saw her. Three of her children had been with her when it happened. They had all been rushed to the hospital. Her kids had suffered only minor injuries, but the mother had died at the hospital.

The article said that she had been a popular and well-loved hair stylist. She had been Christian and known for her warm personality, passion for her family, and dedication to her clients.

I showed the photos to Kiani.

"That's her!" she said.

Wow.

I stared wonderingly at the photo for a bit longer, then my eyes moved up to the top of the page.

The article had been written by a woman named...

Tonya.

—CHAPTER 6—
PROTECTION FROM NEGATIVE SPIRITS

I'm going to pause writing about our experiences with gentle spirits at this point because I feel strongly that now is the time to write about negative or low-level spirits.

This chapter is not just for families of psychic children. The protection techniques listed below work for anyone in need of them.

If you *do* have a child who sees spirits, however, I can't stress enough how *vitally* important it is to create a safe home environment for them; a place where they don't have to hide who they are; a place where they can gently develop and understand their gifts without fear of low-level spirits.

I want to remind you that these are *my personal*

recommendations. They worked for us and continue to work to this day. Chances are, as you get to know your child and/or yourself and grow in knowledge both spiritually and energetically, you will come up with your own twist or take on other great suggestions from people with experience.

Most importantly, you must understand that you and/or your child are *not* alone and that everything will be okay!

God, The Great Spirit, love, the universe, etc. has a plan, and it does *not* involve you and/or your child being miserable.

Now, before I proceed with spiritual protection techniques, I need to mention that the majority of these types of entities are just pests. Like the mosquito, they look for and suck up any negative emotions they can find from humans. Fear, worry, stress, anger, and hatred are delicious flavors to low-levels. If they can make you feel afraid, then that is especially satisfying for them.

But the opposite emotions can send them packing. My sister has the cutest way of dealing with low-levels. She shows them compassion and love and says, "Oh, you poor creature. You must be so miserable. I'm sorry you suffer this way. I'm going to send you a whole bunch of love and a mental hug! Here it comes!"

The entity is instantly repulsed and leaves quickly. I can almost hear it saying, "Ew! Gross! Stop that!"

By tuning into the beautiful, white light of love inside of us and projecting it out either verbally or visually, you can, in a pinch, send these entities into the light and away from you.

In the meantime, let's move into Home Protection.

Step 1
CLEANSING YOUR HOME

What you need:

Faith (If you don't believe in a higher power, chances are you believe in *love,* so tap into it and use it.)

Intention (Take charge, speak with a strong voice, and mean what you say.)

A bundle of dried sage (Other herbs and ingredients in your cabinet can do the trick in a pinch – vinegar, rosemary, cumin, dill, thyme, and basil leaves among them – but sage works extremely well and is easier to work with. Herbs work *wonders* for affecting energy and spirits. The Great Spirit knew exactly what he was doing when creating these plants.)

A bowl (to catch the ashes from the sage)

Light the sage and blow it out to create a gentle flow of smoke. You may have to relight and blow out a few times throughout. Keep a bowl under it to catch any small sparks that fall.

Stand with the sage in the center of the house and say something along these lines (change the words to personally represent your beliefs and values, even if it's only using the force of love):

> *Father Spirit, Creator of Life and Love,*
> *draw close to this family.*
> *We are your children, Father,*
> *and we honor you.*
> *We ask that you bless our family*
> *and bless this house and this property.*
> *Remove all negative spirits from this*
> *home and block them from entering.*

Now address the spirits:

> ***Spirits in this house, listen closely.***
> ***This house and the family who***
> ***live here are under the protection of***
> ***The Father Spirit, The Creator of Life***
> ***and Love. If you do not come here***
> ***with love in your heart,***
> ***then you are trespassing.***
> ***Leave now and never return.***

These are strong words.

Anything negative in your home will immediately flee.

Repeat the last paragraph of the cleansing or a shortened version as you continue.

Now, walk along each wall of the house and through the center of each room, pausing at each window and door. Trace the shape of them with the sage and visualize forming an impenetrable seal of light over each one.

For added benefit, you can also stand in your yard and visualize throwing white light out to the edges of your property and a bit beyond.

When you return to where you started, tamp out the sage (much like a cigar) and take a deep, relaxing breath. You should feel a change in the energy of the house.

I recommend repeating this ritual once every fifteen to thirty days. It will make a huge difference.

Step 2
BEDTIME CLEANSING

I recommend that you sage the bedrooms every night, right before bedtime. You needn't say too much – just a quick prayer of protection and request for a good night's sleep.

Extra safety tips:

Used objects: If you bring a used or crafted object into your home, run it through sage smoke. Objects can carry negative energy or spirit attachments that aren't welcome.

Salt lamps: I learned about salt lamps from a spirit medium. I recommend buying one to keep in each bedroom where it is needed. Low-level entities avoid them.

Herb mixtures: I also recommend placing or

hanging bundles of herbs (I put mine in plastic balls from craft stores) in each room.

Here's an ingredients list that I found to be amazingly affective:

1 tsp dill
1 tsp cumin
1 tsp clove
1 tsp thyme
1 tsp basil
1 tsp rosemary
1 tsp cinnamon
1 bay leaf
A bit of dried sage
1 tsp periwinkle and lavender (if available)

Step 3
CRYSTALS

It is a scientific fact that every living being and inanimate object on this planet vibrates with a frequency of its own.

I often call crystals "medicine stones" because I believe that The Great Spirit gave each of them individual frequencies that can be used to help our bodies and minds in a variety of ways.

When you carry them close to your body, your body responds by trying to match its vibration with those of the crystal. In this way, bad vibrations can affect us as well. Ever notice how being around someone grumpy (even if they don't talk) makes you feel grumpy too? This is how frequencies and vibrations work. When you are aware of them, you are better able to decide what you keep near your body.

There are many crystals and stones that are beneficial to a child with special abilities, but here is a list of my favorites – the absolute *must-haves*. I recommend purchasing the crystals listed below and keeping them close to or on you always. Keep in mind that I only list *some* of their uses. To find out more, check online.

THE AMAZING FIVE

BLACK TOURMALINE
This stone is powerful. It sucks in bad energy and throws it back out as positive. On top of this, it

also absorbs harmful EMF from electronics. It is a comforting stone, sucking up all your sadness and helping you to see the bright side. But most importantly for us, it protects from psychic attacks, from both humans and spirits.

I recommend keeping this stone in the pocket or on the body always. Sleep with it by your head at night, if you can't wear it.

LABRADORITE

This stone protects the aura from the energy of humans and spirits. Being both an empath and an introvert, I never go anywhere without this stone. Even when I'm in a huge crowd, I'm never bothered or drained by others' energy, as I am without it.

Labradorite is especially wonderful for sleep. To me, it feels like someone shutting a door between me and a noisy party going on outside my room and then gently laying a fuzzy, warm blanket across me.

As I've mentioned before, I am also sensitive to spirits, and I've always felt especially vulnerable while sleeping. My guard is down, and for some reason, spirits think that two a.m. is a great time to talk.

One time, I forgot to wear it when I went to bed

and was woken twice by the sound of a ghostly cat howling and a child's voice chattering happily in the next room. I grabbed my stone and bam! Peaceful silence.

SELENITE

This crystal has one of the highest vibrations. Hold it in your hand, and you'll often feel a little warm and tingly where it sits. It can both cleanse and charge your other crystals and needs no cleansing itself.

STAUROLITE

It protects against unwanted spirits, attachments, and negative influences. It also guards against fear, which is an attractive energy to many ghosts.

SPIRIT QUARTZ

This has a strong dampening effect on fear. It protects against unwanted spirits and helps to raise your body's positive vibrations, enhancing your natural ability to connect with angels and other light beings.

CLEANSING YOUR CRYSTALS

We don't just absorb crystal's vibrations; they absorb ours too. This is why cleansing them is important.

To do this, simply set them next to or on top of a selenite crystal, or light your sage bundle and run the crystal through the smoke a couple of times. Remember that selenite also charges the other crystals, which is a bit like giving them a great night's sleep, so they are ready to do their job protecting you.

In my home, I use selenite or a *VibesUp* mat (www.vibesup.com) for charging, which is like selenite times fifty. I also recommend buying one of their "Earth ION pyramids". Negative spirits hate them. They're awesome!

Black Tourmaline doesn't need charged as much as other crystals, but I still do it every week or two anyway. Labradorite needs it every few days, as does spirit quartz and staurolite.

Step 4
PERIWINKLE HERB

As mentioned in Chapter 3, this herb made a

huge difference with my daughter and myself.

(DO NOT EAT IT. I mean for you to *wear it.*)

From what we can tell, negative spirits are only able to get about forty feet from the stuff. They don't like it *at all.*

Now, I'm not saying you won't sense them at a distance, but a distance is *way* better than up close. They will have a *much* harder time harassing a human from that distance.

If you keep your home cleansed on a regular basis, you shouldn't have any problems with negative entities. The periwinkle is an added protection and creates a "cleansed space" around your body, so it's especially important to wear it outside of your home. It keeps dark entities out of your body space and stops them from following you or your child home, which I've had experience with as well.

You can purchase vials and the herb online and make your own amulets or search for someone who sells them pre-made.

ONE FINAL NOTE

If you've done all the above and *still* feel a

negative entity in your home, then chances are you have a spirit attachment, human or otherwise. It doesn't happen often, but it's not unheard of. There are energy cords that form between people we love, work with, and sometimes even just have an intense moment with. These invisible cords are formed by thoughts and emotions and can come from both people or just one. They can even form online, from a heated conversation.

You can learn more about these cords and how to cut the negative ones in Chapter 22, but first, I have some more stories to share.

—CHAPTER 7—
THE BOY AND THE BOX

After the ghost of "The Warm Lady" left, a few months went by with the usual random appearances of gentle spirits, both animal and human, with nothing noteworthy to mention.

By this time, Kiani and I had truly perfected the art of home protection, which I wrote about in the last chapter. We hadn't had an obnoxious or bad spirit enter our home since our move, which was wonderful. We felt like we could just relax and enjoy the "ghostly scenery", as you might say.

I will mention a couple interesting events that happened to us before moving on.

Kiani came home from a weekend visit with her dad and described seeing two apparitions, which I found interesting – partly because she felt like they were the same spirit, but mainly because this was the first time she had ever seen a spirit visibly affect its environment.

One was a figure of what looked like a man, who entered through her bedroom door. She described him as a black, human shape with thousands of bright purple sparkles dancing inside the blackness. Quite beautiful.

She said that she had been feeling scared to sleep alone that night, and as she was thinking about this, the figure walked through the door and toward her bed, crossing over a rug on the way there. She said that the rug went down under his feet as he walked, leaving foot-shaped impressions, which glittered with purple sparkles for a couple seconds before fading.

The figure then walked over to her bed and sat down, turning to face her. His body formed an indention on the blanket.

"I didn't feel like he was bad or anything," Kiani told me. "But the bed moving kind of freaked me out a bit."

"What did you do?" I asked her.

"I whispered 'hi' to him and then hid under the covers."

She said later that she thought he must have

showed up to watch over her as she slept because she doesn't remember feeling afraid after that, just falling asleep peacefully.

The next day, she saw another man, which she believed to be the same man, watching her from the corner of her dad's kitchen. This time, he was in solid form, and she described his appearance.

"He was kind of old, with a wrinkly face and white stubble on his chin. He had a cowboy hat on and a vest and boots."

She saw this man a few more times in solid form at our house later. Each time, he was just casually walking in or out of rooms, which was typical behavior for the ghosts that Kiani was used to seeing.

(The cowboy spirit continued to connect with us over the next few months. The following February, he finally revealed himself as one of our spirit guides, which I'll go into later.)

The next spirit to visit us however, was *far* from typical.

The first time she saw the boy was when we were coming home from shopping. As she was walking upstairs to our loft apartment, she noticed him looking down at us over the balcony rail.

Then she saw him a second time – bent down, peering curiously into my pet ball python's tank.

"He looks like he's about maybe twelve or thirteen, and he was dressed weird," she told me when I asked her what he looked like.

My ears perked up at this. I have long been obsessed with fashion of the bygone eras, especially the 1700s and 1800s. Maybe this was an older ghost. I asked her for more details and laughed a little at her struggle to describe what he was wearing (Kiani knows little about vintage clothing).

"He had a long vest on, with lots of big buttons going down it...and a shirt on under it with long sleeves, but they were weird, like...all bubbly."

"You mean puffy?"

"Yeah. And his pants were funny-looking. They only came to right under his knees, and there were buttons on those too, on the bottom. And he was wearing long socks that didn't stay up well and these...um...buckles on his shoes. Big ones."

My eyes got huge.

"Kiani! You just described colonial clothing. Do you know what that is?"

"No."

"You described boys' clothing from the 1700s –

George Washington's time. That was almost three hundred years ago."

"Whoa," was the reply.

"We should try to talk to him with the spirit box next time you see him," I suggested.

The spirit box is a neat little invention. You may have seen it before, if you've ever watched a ghost hunting show. We had tried one a couple months back, when a friend loaned hers to us.

It's a little radio with an antenna that's designed to scan through radio stations at super-fast speeds. The concept behind it is that spirits speak on a frequency that's hard for humans to hear. But radios are supposed to be able to pick up these voices. It scans quickly through the stations – too fast to hear more than a split-second of DJs speaking and music notes. So, if you *do* hear a word and especially *two or more* words of a sentence, then you're making true contact.

(I must caution you, if you plan to use a spirit box or any spirit communication device. Be aware that if you use it in a home that isn't blessed and sealed with sage and white light, it is possible that you will attract the attention of spirits you would not want in your home. If you plan to use it outside your blessed home space, such as on a ghost tour, be sure that you keep periwinkle, black tourmaline, or black obsidian on your person or in your car so that you don't bring unwelcome visitors home with you.)

In our few days with the borrowed box, we had a couple interesting moments. My favorite was when we asked about spirit cats, and the box said, "Cat...cat...kitty...cat...meow." When we jokingly asked what a ghost cat might eat, a man's voice promptly replied, "Just give him some bread."

(I stupidly didn't think to record this session, but we definitely got the boy's voice recorded in a later chapter).

The second interesting session with the box seemed like it was going nowhere. All we got was static and cut-off words from DJs and commercials.

But then something happened that served as a reminder of how effective and important it is to keep your home cleansed and protected.

I felt the unmistakable presence of something dark and negative begin to enter the room. I opened my mouth to remark on this when a deep, male voice over the box said, "F**k!" Then, quickly, the presence vanished.

I feel strongly that whatever it was failed to come in due to the protection we keep on the house and especially the bedrooms. The window directly to my right was lined with bits of sage along the sill, and the nightstand held a black tourmaline and a periwinkle amulet.

A few days later, we got our chance to talk to the boy. Before continuing, I will explain why this boy is especially unusual. Maybe it's because of how long he's been around – I don't know – but the kid has a knack for moving objects, and he does it a lot.

Before the first spirit box session with him, he had moved two objects. First was a half-eaten bag of chips, pushed gently up to Kiani's leg as she played on her phone. Then, in much the same manner, he pushed a little toy dog toward Kiani as she was playing.

On the day we first heard him, Kiani had seen him again, and I decided to give the box a shot.

I was still rather new to it and not used to how loud the static sounds were. I sat there, fussing with it and trying out a pair of earphones, to see if it sounded better.

"Ugh," I complained, "these earphones are awful."

I closed my eyes and started to listen again, then was suddenly startled by Kiani tapping me hard on the leg. I looked at her, and she pointed behind me, wide-eyed.

When I turned around, I saw a few necklaces and a pair of earphones three feet behind me, swinging gently back and forth on their wall hook.

(I didn't make the connection at the time, but someone was obviously trying to be helpful by pointing out my second pair of earphones.)

I yanked the first pair of earphones out of my ears and looked back at Kiani.

"Something lifted them!" she said, amazement in her voice. "I saw them being picked up!"

I turned back around and stared in awe as the last bit of movement came to a stop.

I quickly plugged the stereo into the box, so we both could hear, and said, "Someone just moved the necklaces behind me. Who did that?"

A couple seconds of static was followed by the voice of a preteen boy. "I did."

"What's your name?" I asked him.

"Weston," the boy's voice said, then back to the static.

We couldn't get him to say anything else at this

point, so we had to give it up for the day.

After this, he continued in his cute attempts to play with Kiani. He spun the hamster wheel as she reached for her hamster, pushed another toy toward her while she played, and so on.

She kept seeing him too, in solid, misty, and light-colored shadow forms. His favorite times to show up were when we were being silly, talking about interesting subjects, or doing fun activities as a family.

He never did and never has shown himself or moved anything downstairs, however. It's like he understands that he would scare my mom.

Once, I managed to contact him using my tarot cards (as I did in The Warm Lady chapter). He had been with us a while, and I wanted to know what he wanted and if he needed help.

His response was that he loved our home because we are kind and funny, and all the pets fascinate him (we have many). He especially likes Kiani and thinks she's entertaining.

I talked about him moving objects, and he expressed a lot of worry and shame on the subject. "Is it bad to move objects? I can't help it. Please don't be mad," was the strong impression I got.

(Looking back on this reaction later, it became obvious to me that he most likely scared the living crap out of the families he'd visited over the years. It's no wonder he responded that way. He wanted to be with us and enjoy our company, not scare us to death.)

The tarot session ended with me telling him that he most likely has family waiting for him somewhere and that if he wanted to go to them, my Guardian Spirit would lead him to where he needed to go. I told him he was a good kid and that he was welcome here, if he decided to stay instead. The choice was his.

Well, as you can probably guess, he chose to stay for a little while longer.

I think what amused me the most about Weston was his love of stories. He always seemed to show up when I was telling the kids about something funny or interesting that happened to me or when I would read my writing out loud to check for errors. Kiani would see an outline of him standing in the doorway, leaning casually into the frame, like any preteen boy would if he wants to *hear* the stories but not appear *too* interested.

—CHAPTER 8—
THE TRAVELLING PENNY

Weston, the ghost boy from the 1700s, continued to make his presence known over the next couple months. Objects around my daughter, Kiani, continued to move regularly; a feather, jewelry pliers (these were moved a few feet from a dresser to my bed while we were out shopping), toys, and pet mice furniture among them.

We had already determined that he was a shy and respectful boy, drawn to laughter, animals, and stories. But we also discovered that he had a sense of humor as well.

Once, when we were watching a movie, Kiani saw the boy's arm emerge from a wall and reach slowly toward our cat, to gently *boop* her on the nose. The cat responded to this in the typical semi-startled blink that accompanies being *booped*.

(At this time, we were starting to pay attention to our pets' reaction to what Kiani sees, and it was cool. They see everything my daughter does, and it gives a nice sense of validation to the stuff we experience.)

As you can imagine, we were growing quite used to having the boy around. When a spirit is as gentle as this kid is, you can't help but feel some fondness toward him.

What we didn't realize, though, is how much he cared for us in return.

One day, I got some bad financial news of a sort. A big chunk of my income wouldn't be coming in for a long time, if ever again. The kids and I had been dependent on it for a lot of our needs. My mom offered to help, of course, but that day was stressful for me. I didn't want to have to ask her for help.

I remember crying and the kids asking what was wrong. I explained the best I could, then I went outside to sit on the porch for a while – a place I often go to find some peace.

A few minutes later, Kiani came out the front door and sat down next to me. She pulled her phone out and started to play a game on it.

All was quiet for a bit.

"Hey!" she exclaimed suddenly.

I turned to see her touching the top of her head, looking baffled.

"What?" I asked her.

"Something just fell on my head. Maybe it was a bug or something?"

She took a few seconds to look for whatever had fallen on her then,

"Look!" she said, holding up something small. "It's a penny!"

I laughed.

"What the heck?" I replied. "That's so weird!"

"Think it was Weston?"

"Probably," I answered. "Kind of a funny thing for him to do, though. I wonder if he just wants your attention tonight."

When we walked back inside, we discovered that the penny was only one coin in a handful. Just inside the door was another penny, then a dime on the stairs, and another toward the top. We followed them in a trail up the stairs and to the source – a little jar of change that I kept on a coffee table.

It didn't take long for us to figure out what had

happened. Talk of money problems, my tears, and the kids' concern must have upset Weston. I could almost hear him thinking, *Look! Here's a little jar of coins! Surely, this could help, right? Maybe I'll remind them about it.*

I would have given anything to have seen with my own eyes his amazing effort to carry a handful of them downstairs. Such an incredibly sweet thing to do.

—CHAPTER 9—
LUNA AND THE TUNA

Tragedy struck in October 2017.

My elderly golden retriever approached me one morning with the deepest, saddest expression on her face. Her head hung low, as if it felt too heavy for her, and her eyes were pleading as she stared at me.

"What's wrong, old lady?" I asked her.

It occurred to me that she hadn't been eating as much over the past few days and was slower to get up.

I called the vet and brought her in for an exam. They took some blood and ran some tests. Then they called with the bad news.

She had developed cancer of the spleen, which had ruptured, causing internal bleeding. This was why she had become weak, even to the point of finding food to be too much effort. Surgery would be costly, painful, and pointless, since the cancerous blood from the ruptured organ was now circulating throughout her body.

"How long does she have?" I asked the vet.

"Not long," came the reply. "I would say no more than a week, at best."

She explained that if left to run its course, the bleeding would intensify to the point where she would bleed to death internally.

I didn't like the sound of this. What if she died alone, while we were sleeping? Supposedly, it wasn't painful to die this way, as they pass out from blood loss before passing, but the vet also said that sometimes, they know what is happening to them and feel fear before they pass out. I didn't want that. No one should die alone and afraid, especially my loyal and sweet family dog.

I asked her how many days I had before she reached that danger point. She said no more than two days.

I was shocked.

How had this happened so fast? One minute, she was fine, and the next, she was dying.

It hit all of us hard. We cried and loved on her

and cried some more.

It didn't take long to decide what I had to do, however. I arranged for an in-home euthanasia in two days' time. The vet would come to our home and give her a powerful painkiller and sedative, and once she was asleep, they would inject a drug to stop her heart.

It was the most comfortable, pain-free death imaginable, and she was worth it. She had loved us with all her heart, and I wanted her to have the best.

As soon as I made the appointment, I went to work on her body, using some of the alternative healing techniques I had learned over the last couple years. They worked. She became stronger, her appetite increased, and she was able to move better.

This made it easier to pamper her those last two days. She ate all her favorite human foods with us, slept in our beds, and got all the cuddles and doggie massages her heart desired.

Kiani and I wondered what would happen when she passed. Would she know that she had died? Would Kiani see her? Would her spirit stay with us or move on?

What we kept forefront in our minds was that she wasn't going to cease to exist. She was simply transitioning from one form to another. This gave us comfort in the days and weeks to come.

When her transition day arrived, it turned out to be even more beautiful and peaceful than I imagined. We fed her bits of tuna and even pizza (something she had never been allowed to eat in her life) off a plate while we waited for her to get sleepy. I have never seen her so happy! Her last apparent thought before she fell asleep and before the final injection was, *Yes! That bite! The big piece! Oh, yum!*

When she closed her eyes, that giant piece of pizza was still sticking out the side of her mouth. It was truly beautiful.

Our questions on whether we would see her again were soon answered.

That night, Kiani and I were sitting in my room, playing on our devices, when Kiani suddenly sat bolt upright.

"Mommy! I just saw Luna!"

"What? What happened?!"

"I looked up from playing for a second and saw her back and tail. She walked past me and over there." She pointed to the left end of my bed. "But I looked away because I forgot she was dead and then I realized what I saw and looked again. I can't see anything now, but I saw her! Solid form!"

She was grinning from ear to ear, and I couldn't help smiling with her.

Just then, one of our cats, who had been sleeping next to Kiani, suddenly stood up and stared in the direction that Kiani had said Luna had walked.

Her eyes were bright and focused as she stared at the spot for a few seconds. Then she jumped down and walked over to it. She began pawing at the carpet and walking back and forth, much like she used to do while greeting Luna; that gentle glide that cats do along your legs.

"Look!" Kiani said. "I think she sees her!"

I had to agree with her.

Two more incidents happened over the next few days.

While Luna was still alive, it had always been her habit to go downstairs, into my son's room, when Kiani and I would leave on errands.

A couple days after Luna's transition, Kiani and I came back from a store run and went into my son's room to bring him his requested ice cream.

He told us that a minute or so after we left, his pet bunny had startled, ran into a wall of his cage, and then started thumping his foot in alarm, staring at a spot near the end of his bed (the place Luna used to lay in).

I told my son that I felt quite sure it had been Luna. He blinked at me in amazement and then nodded, smiling.

"I think you're right!" he said.

It made me happy to see him smiling like that. It wasn't just Luna having been there. It was also his second encounter with a spirit (he didn't remember the first one, which had been the playset being lifted off the ground a few years ago), and he was thrilled about that. Before this, he was used to just hearing stories from Kiani and myself.

After this incident, Kiani saw Luna a couple more times in a mist-like form, walking around the house.

Then I experienced something I wasn't expecting at all.

Luna's favorite food of all time was tuna. She always thought of herself as more of a cat than a dog and had been especially excited over the cans of tuna we occasionally fed to the cats (of which she was always given some).

One morning, there were zero cans of tuna left in the house. The last two had been fed to Luna on the day she passed, and what remained of the tuna had been cleaned up days ago.

But as I was standing in my kitchen, trying to think what to cook, I was suddenly overwhelmed by the strong odor of tuna fish. It was so strong, in fact, that it was as if someone had opened a fresh can of it and passed it under my nose!

How could I be smelling tuna? Any remains had been thrown out a while ago. Then I suddenly recalled reading that spirits are often accompanied by scents that were important to them when alive.

I dropped down into a squat and held my hands out to the space around me.

"Luna," I said softly, "I miss you, baby girl. I hope you know how much I love you."

Tears slid down my cheeks. I took a shaky breath, then continued.

"You can stay here with us, if you like, or you can go into the light and wait for us there. Whatever you want to do, okay?"

I felt and heard nothing, but the smell was as

strong as ever.

After a few moments, I stood up and the scent faded.

We think that it took her a few days to understand what had happened. She must have left her body and then just kept right on doing what she always did.

I feel that at some point, she thought, *Why doesn't anyone see me? Why does no one talk to me or touch me?*

I think that when she realized what had happened, she came to me for direction. I believe that her soul understood what I told her, and she decided.

Luna visited us twice after this, always accompanied by the smell of tuna.

One day, we came home from a trip to a pet store, and I opened a bag of little, green bone treats in the kitchen. They also used to be one of Luna's favorites, but I hadn't thought of her in a while, having been so busy.

Well, when I opened that bag of green bones and stepped a few feet away, to the top of the stairs, there came again that overwhelming smell that accompanies her: tuna fish!

After my initial shock at smelling her again, I came out of it, placed one of the bones on the floor, and said, "Here, Luna! Treat!"

At that point, Kiani and I heard the distinctive sound of her collar tinkling a couple times. I hope that food has a spirit replica of itself in the spirit world! Wouldn't that be neat? Maybe it does. After all, many cultures around the world leave gifts of food for the spirits. Maybe they know something I don't.

Another day, I was especially missing her and expressed some regrets about how I felt I hadn't truly appreciated her enough for all that she did and wished I could tell her. That night, Kiani and I both dreamed of her. She came to us and put her head in our laps, and we held her and cuddled her for a long time. I believe this was her way of saying, "It's okay, family. I loved my life with you. I would do it all over again if I could. Don't be sad. I'm crossed over now, but I'll come visit you sometimes, and when you're ready to cross over one day, I'll be waiting for you."

I feel, without an ounce of a doubt, that I will see her again. I once read something online that makes me tear up to this day.

It said that when we pass into the light – into the place where we are greeted by our loved ones – we are quickly rushed upon by a crowd of our pets that have passed on before us. It said that, in typical animal fashion, our pets are the first to see and hear us coming and the first to get to us. Our human loved ones have to wait patiently behind the crowd of wagging tails, delighted meows, chirping, and wing-flapping before they can get in for that long-awaited hug.

Can't you just picture that? What an amazing moment.

—CHAPTER 10—
THE MAN IN THE BOWLER HAT

"Ghost hunting" is rather a silly choice of words, when you think about it. A group of highly visible people trying to sneak up on invisible people and catch them doing visible things.

It had been over a year since my daughter, Kiani, had told me about her ability to see these invisible people, but up until this point, I hadn't taken her out to a haunted location.

After our golden retriever passed away, though, I started thinking of ways to get our minds off it. A haunted tour might be just the solution.

I didn't want anything too creepy or with a violent past. I hoped to find a cute little Victorian house in town somewhere. As it turned out, I was in luck because I found one right when I needed it.

Normally used for weddings and special events,

the beautiful 1890s home had just opened to the local paranormal society. For fifteen dollars, you and about twenty others could tour parts of the home in small groups led by a few members of the paranormal society. They even gave you hands-on access to some of their ghost-hunting equipment, which included K2 meters (EMF detectors) and heat sensors.

Kiani and I packed up our little spirit box and a pair of headphones, and off we went.

The house was adorable. It was a beautifully maintained, white Victorian with gingerbread-sided towers and a welcoming front porch.

We were shown in by one of the home's coordinators and led inside to wait.

While waiting, I read through a little flier on the home's history. It had been built by a doctor who had seen many of his patients inside the front area of the home. It talked a bit about him and his family and a few others who came after. Nothing traumatic had happened to any of its residents, other than a kitchen fire in which no one had been hurt. A few people had died in the home of various health problems or old age, including the doctor and his sister.

I set the flier down and looked at Kiani, who stood quietly next to me, listening to the people talking around her. I couldn't help but feel excited and a little proud. I knew if there was anything to see in this house, *she would see it.*

When the time came, we were separated into small groups of six to eight people. The first room was a small "sewing room" in the back of the house. Nothing happened in this room except for a man's voice over the spirit box commenting on the equipment. (I wish I could recall what it said right now. This is one of the reasons I am glad to be getting this down in writing. Memories fade over time.)

After this, we headed into the front parlor, where the doctor was said to have had his office. We hit the ghostly jackpot in this room.

The spirit box came to life with a man's voice, who responded to the paranormal society guide's questions in one- or two-word sentences. The K2 meters went nuts as well, and the lights of the devices moved in time with the man speaking.

From the answers he gave, the guide was convinced that it was the doctor. The spirit even spoke about having terrible migraines, which coincided with the way he died.

About this time, Kiani spoke up and said she'd just seen a man in a bowler hat walk past us in solid form.

The group turned to my daughter in surprise.

"She sees dead people," I told them, cracking a grin.

They seemed quite pleased to hear this and kept watching her carefully throughout the rest of the tour.

Just before we left the doctor's office, Kiani felt a spirit touch her foot, and we mentioned this as well.

"That felt so weird!" she said, eyes wide. "It felt tingly and kind of cold."

(This was the first time a spirit had touched her).

After this room came the doctor's sister's old room, which was strangely quiet. Even the spirit box was a no-go.

Once outside again, though, Kiani spotted three shadow people walking through the yard and followed them briefly, only to see them vanish at the edges. She also told me later that she'd seen several orbs flying through the house the whole time.

When the tour ended, the guides had everyone

stand in a large circle and each take a moment to talk about anything they had seen or heard.

Oh, boy, I thought. *Here we go.* If the rest didn't know about Kiani, they would soon.

It went about how I expected. Most people hadn't seen or heard anything. One mentioned an odd creaking sound, and another said they saw something out of the corner of their eye.

Then came our turn. Kiani and I looked at each other for a second, then I explained what we had experienced. It felt like it took forever to recount, especially to a shy introvert like myself, but the surprised and smiling faces of the people listening made it worth the telling.

What tickled me the most was right when the group started to disperse. We were immediately approached by the paranormal society group members, who didn't waste a second in questioning Kiani.

"So, you saw a lot tonight, huh?"

"You saw the same ghost I've seen a lot of – the man in the bowler hat. Was he wearing a brown vest? Pleasant? Nice-looking face? Ha! That's the one. How cool!"

"Do you see ghosts a lot?"

"You and your daughter should come to more of our events. We'd love to have you."

We did our best to answer all the questions and then said our goodbyes.

"Did you have fun?" I asked Kiani, once we were back inside the car.

"Yes!" came the enthusiastic reply. "Can we do that again?"

I grinned at her. "I don't see why not."

—CHAPTER 11—
THE CORPSE IN THE CLOSET

In late November of 2017, Kiani returned home from visiting her dad with an unsettling story.

She said that she had been playing with her stepcousins in one of the bedrooms when she looked up to see a woman standing in the closet.

She described the woman as being in solid form, with foggy eyes (like those of a corpse). She wore a white nightdress, and her black hair hung straight and long past her waist.

As if this wasn't disturbing enough on its own, Kiani also described how the woman's head hung loose on her shoulders from an elongated neck (presumably broken and stretched from a hanging).

"It was so creepy, Mommy!" she told me, her eyes wide. "She was looking right at me too!"

"Were you wearing your periwinkle amulet?"

"Yes! Why didn't it work?"

I was thoughtful for a minute.

From our experience with the herb, negative spirits could still be seen at a distance, but not one had been able to get closer than about thirty feet.

I asked her to describe the distance between her and the deceased woman, and I estimated it to be about fourteen feet.

I knew that spirits often required quite a bit of energy to manifest. What if the woman had drawn strength from the large group of loud, energetic children? What if this energy had been more than enough, therefore enabling her to get as close as she did?

I told Kiani my theory.

She pursed her lips in consideration. "I think you're right," she admitted. "My cousins *are* super hyper."

I laughed and then hugged her.

"I'm so sorry, honey. That must have been scary for you."

"It was!"

"How'd you handle it, though?" I asked her. I wondered if she had remembered and used some of the techniques I taught her. "Did you ignore her or pray about it?"

"No, she was hard to ignore. I prayed about it in my head and then imagined white light coming from my body. She left."

I hugged her again.

"Wow! Kiani! I am *so proud of you*! You handled that like a *pro!*"

She grinned at me.

"Yeah, I guess I did," came the reply.

—CHAPTER 12—
HOUSE OF LIGHT

Apparently, our house has a nickname in the spirit world. I'd picked up on the phrase "house of light" in a card reading a few months back but had forgotten all about it – until we had an unexpected visit from a passing spirit in January.

The month before had been a time of excitement and joy for us. We adopted a puppy through a reputable breeder, and he finally shipped to us on the eighth. We were so excited! He turned out to be the most adorable, loving little guy too!

We also had quite a few family members visit us for Christmas, so as you can imagine, we didn't notice much spirit activity for a while.

In the middle of January, though, it started to pick back up again. Kiani started seeing figures walking past and occasional flashes of light here and there.

One evening, I got in the car to pick my son up from his martial arts class and felt someone in the car with me. It felt a bit like a grumpy old person. Not harmful, just angry and unpleasant. Not the type of spirit you would feel comfy around.

(It couldn't get into the house, so it decided to lurk in the front yard instead. Because of this incident, I started including our property as well as our house in my cleansing blessing rituals.)

I opted to ignore it and went on my way. I didn't feel it once my son got into the car—

(My son throws out a natural white light energy. There is something special about him, and I hope to find out more one day.)

—and since these types of spirits can't get into our house, I forgot all about it once I was upstairs.

A little while later, I was sitting on my bed, playing on my phone, when I saw a cream-colored human figure walk past my doorway a couple times.

I remarked on this because I don't usually see spirits. That's mostly my daughter's department.

Kiani replied that she'd seen the same figure a few minutes ago.

I put my phone down and said out loud, "Is there

a spirit here? Can you come over here a minute? We'd like to talk with you."

"Whoa!" breathed Kiani. "I just saw a streak of light and two orbs come toward us!"

I immediately grabbed my tarot cards and spirit communication gadgets.

The spirit box was drained of batteries. It was odd because it shouldn't have been, but yet, not odd with the amount of gentle spirits we get in the house. Spirits often affect electronics this way.

The Ovilus (which reads energy in the air and tried to match words to the frequencies) was working, though. I turned it on and set it down. It quickly piped up with the words, "little magic."

I picked up my tarot cards, shuffled them, and asked the spirit a few questions.

"Who are you?"

Man.

"Why are you here?"

Safe.

House of Light.

Peaceful here.

Something outside isn't nice.

The Ovilus spoke up again and said, "Safe."

"I get the feeling that you are a kind spirit," I

said gently. "You're welcome to stay here until you feel better."

There was no reply, but I didn't feel I needed one. It made me happy to think that our home was so full of warm, spiritual light that passing spirits could come here to rest and think. Perhaps this spirit had encountered the one I felt outside and came into our home to escape it.

The gentle spirit's replies also explained the variety of passing forms and shapes my daughter sees on such a regular basis, as well being a reminder of how important it is to keep our home protected.

We had a lot of these gentle visitors over the next few months. At first, I didn't know how to help them, or even if I should try. Eventually, after talking with other spirit mediums and reading a lot of their written work, I changed tactics. I hung a hand-written letter up on the back of my bedroom door for any passing spirits to read. It explained how and why they should go into the light and recommended that they visit the funeral home down the street from me, where the light was always available behind the many newly passed spirits in the building.

I also learned how to create the light myself, but I have to say, it's quite strange to create something useful you can't see! I feel like I'd imagine a blind person would, leading a seeing person across the street! Because I can't see the light I create, I have to rely on what Kiani sees during the rescues and my intuitive senses, which can pick up on the lack of energy in the air afterward and the lack of spirit activity over the following days.

There was one time when we had *so* many ghosts in the house that I decided to work with Kiani on visualizing a gigantic, white archway of light, right in the center of the house! Then I asked our spirit guides and angels to do the rest, while we focused on the visual of the doorway. It was quite an experience! I don't think I've had had goosebumps that much in my life! When we finished, the house felt *empty and quiet* and stayed that way for a couple weeks.

—CHAPTER 13—
THE MOLDY MAN

Despite its slow start, the first month of 2018 turned out to be the most paranormally active month yet for my daughter and me. January hasn't ended yet, and I have at least three new stories to share.

I don't include every little detail because frankly, it's a lot – sometimes brief and often repetitive – but there is and will always be something new and interesting to write about.

Not too long after the "House of Light" encounter, Kiani and I were tucked into bed and ready to fall asleep (though she has her own room, she has slept in mine since she was a baby, due to her ability to see spirits).

We were feeling relaxed and starting to drift off when we heard a soft click and the tinkling notes of a music box.

"What is that music?" Kiani wondered out loud.

I knew she wasn't all that familiar with music boxes, but I certainly was.

"It's a music box," I told her. "Weird."

We tried again to sleep but kept hearing faint, unidentifiable noises from my bedroom and living room.

"Oh, for Pete's sake," I said, feeling tired and not in the mood for a ghost party.

I stood up and spoke to the air around me.

"Hey, spirit people and such, would you mind settling down and being quiet? Time may not mean much where you are, but Kiani and I are trying to sleep. Thank you!"

They must have heard us because we didn't hear anything after that and slept quite well.

A few days after the ghostly party crashers, I experienced another something that seemed to validate that I have something called "Clairessence", which is the psychic ability to smell scents and odors from the spirit world.

My sense of smell has always been my stronger sense, so I guess it shouldn't surprise me, but on this night, I learned that not every spirit smells pleasant.

On this night, my kids had a few friends over. They were playing board games, and I was helping them organize them. I started to smell what I can only describe as rotting, wet clothes. It was so strong, in fact, that I almost gagged.

Instead, I held my breath and looked around at the table of boys, wondering why I didn't smell it before. But I assumed, logically, that it must be coming from one of them.

After a few moments, though, the odor vanished, and I could focus again. The fresh air lasted a good half-hour, and then it came back again.

This time, I was determined to figure out where it was coming from so that I could sit farther away from the culprit.

Don't laugh (or do!), but I stood up and, as casually and nonchalantly as I could, walked around the table from kid to kid, interacting with them and cracking jokes. I had the "cool mom" reputation to uphold, after all, and didn't want to ruin that by being obvious about what I was doing.

But once done with my sly, sniffing detective work, I was even more baffled. *None* of the kids smelled bad. *Not one.* I remember being so baffled that I even walked into the bathroom and sniffed my own clothing. *Nothing*.

It began to annoy me. I sighed and shook my head, then walked out of the bathroom and toward the stairs.

And there it was *again!*

As I stood there, scowling, with my hands on my hips, Kiani motioned to me from the bedroom, just a few feet to my left.

"Mommy, come here!" she whispered.

I stepped close to her.

"I just saw a man's legs walk past you. Not his torso, just his legs."

"You did?" I whispered back. "What was he wearing?"

"It looked like pants and shiny shoes...fancy ones."

That was all the detail she could give me, but I *knew* this gentleman spirit must have been what I had been smelling all night.

Later, after speaking with a few psychic friends of mine online, I discovered that that moldy, rotten clothes smell was quite common while in the presence of the departed.

Mystery solved.

Unfortunately, it also came with the realization that I will just have to toughen up and quit being such a wuss over bad odors. I have a feeling this won't be the last of them.

—CHAPTER 14—
THE FEATHER

We were used to spirits moving objects around our house, but something happened one day that seriously surprised us.

Kiani had a necklace she wore often. It was a little, green fluorite amulet, which I gave her to help with focus and concentration.

One day, she was playing a board game with a friend who was visiting our house. I'll refer to him as "Jason". During the game, Jason complained about his lack of focus lately, especially in school. His complaints made Kiani's lack of focus seem like nothing in comparison.

The next Sunday, I took Kiani shopping with me at a Target down the street. Later that night, we noticed that her amulet had vanished, along with the chain it was on. I assumed it must have broken off during the day, while we were out. I wasn't too upset about it, since I owned a few other stones that would do in a pinch. I told her not to let it bother her, and we went to bed.

A few days later, Jason came over again to play. As he stood there, talking to us, I noticed he had a necklace on. When I looked closer, I was shocked.

"Oh my God!" I exclaimed. "That looks just like the necklace Kiani lost a few days ago!"

Jason grinned. "Isn't it cool? I found it on the floor at Target."

"The Target just down the street?" I asked.

"Yep."

"Was this last Sunday?"

"Yes, actually."

I could hardly believe it. It wasn't a common amulet. The chances of someone with an identical crystal and chain dropping theirs at the same Target on the same day was extremely slim. It had to have been Kiani's.

"Well, I'll be damned," I said, obvious wonder in my voice. "Kiani lost hers," I explained to him, "and we were there the same day. I think you're meant to have it!" I smiled at him.

His eyes got huge for a moment, and he smiled

back.

"Wow, really? Well, I guess so, then!"

This amazed me so much that I started thinking seriously about all the incredible "coincidences" in my life. How many of them weren't coincidences at all?

I believe that humans have Guardian Spirits (angels), but what if that wasn't all? What if we have a whole bunch of gentle spirits working on our behalf every day? What if our spirits communicated with and worked with other people's companion spirits?

I had heard of spirit guides but had never thought much about my own or my daughter's. Perhaps it was high time.

I purchased a recommended book about connecting with your spirit guides, and two days later, it was in my mailbox. Excited, I snatched it out and brought it inside, placing it on my coffee table before walking into the bathroom.

As I washed my hands, I looked up and there, on my vest, was a little, white feather.

I had read somewhere that angels leave feathers as a form of communication. I thought of that as I looked at it, shrugged, then set it aside to think about later.

Soon after this, I experienced something that completely blew my mind and explained the meaning of the feather.

—CHAPTER 15—
THE EARTHQUAKE

Before I continue, I need to tell you about something life-changing that happened to me when I was twenty-five.

As I mentioned in a previous chapter, I consider myself a Native American Spiritual these days, but I was raised Christian. Seventh-Day Adventist, to be exact. Adventists are bible-based. They believe in the Saturday Sabbath, the resurrection, and that the dead *stay* dead. No such thing as ghosts.

I was naturally a spiritual child, and I can tell you with all honesty that amazing things have happened to me (and my family) regularly since I was young.

But when I was eleven, I started to struggle with the true identity of God. I *knew* He existed. I had felt His energy and even briefly communicated with

Him since I was four years old.

What I felt, without a doubt, was that He was loving and kind, not angry or judgmental. His energy felt fatherly to me – not the type who yells, hits, or withholds affection, but the type of dad who listens and hugs you after a bad day at school or talks your Mom into easing up on the no-sugar rule this week, since the kiddo had such a hard day. Let's go get ice cream!

Words are powerful. They can pull you up to great heights, or they can shatter your world.

When I was eleven, one of my older sisters shattered mine. I walked into a room and found her crying. When I asked what was wrong, she said she was worried she wasn't going to be allowed into Heaven.

I was confounded. *My sweet sister? Not make it to Heaven?*

"Why?" I asked her.

Her reply was that she felt like she ate too much.

I was speechless. How could the God that I knew and loved be capable of keeping my sister out of Heaven over something so trivial? She eats one too many doughnuts, and *bam! Sorry, lady. Can't let you through.*

That just couldn't be possible!

But...she was much older than me. She must know something I didn't, right?

Wrong.

But I didn't know that at the time.

Over the next few years, I grew more confused and sad. As spiritual as I was, I could *not* make what I knew of God in my heart match up with the God that people said He was. The Bible was no help either. The horrible things I read in there (mixed in with the good) just made it worse for me.

Add the fact that I was such an unusual person in many ways, and it all amounted to one miserable, confused human. I was at a complete loss.

Finally, when I was twenty-five, I made up my mind. I decided that since I couldn't make sense of God, I would just *give Him up*. I stopped talking to Him, stopped praying, and completely ignored my spiritual side.

And what followed was the darkest year of my life. I don't remember ever feeling so lost and sad.

But one day, something happened that wiped it all away.

I was walking toward the staircase, which led to

my bedroom. But as my hand touched the railing, the house around me vanished.

In my mind, I was standing outside, in the middle of a hardened, dry desert. Encircling me was a huge crowd of people. Every one of them was looking straight at me, and all of them wore expressions varying between concern, anger, arrogance, and pity. Some of the more emotional ones even had an arm raised, pointing at me.

Their voices said:

"You are not worthy of God's love."

"God will punish you if you act that way!"

"You can't do that. It's not normal, and God would not approve."

"You say you love God, but you don't even go to church."

"You are not good enough!"

Then, out of nowhere, the ground began to shake violently. It opened around me, and the crowd of people tumbled down into the black chasm and vanished out of sight.

I stood there on my tiny piece of untouched earth, in awe of what had just happened.

I turned carefully and slowly in a circle. The land was gone not just where the people had been, but everywhere. All except where I stood. I saw nothing but blackness to the end of the Earth and blackness below, where the crowd had been swallowed by the dark.

Then I looked up.

Coming from the sky was the most beautiful, warm, white light I had ever seen, and I recognized it instantly.

It was God, The Goddess, The Father, The Great Spirit, The Source, The Creator, The Universe, The Force that holds everything together.

It was m*y friend*.

And the second I recognized this, the scene in my head vanished. I was back at the foot of the stairs, holding onto the railing.

I gasped and let go. Tears streamed down my face, and I didn't bother to stop them. I cried with a glorious combination of relief and happiness.

"Thank you," I said. "I understand now. I know you're there. Let's start from scratch, you and me? Teach me about the *real* you?"

And He did.

Years have passed, but I know I will never stop learning because The Great Spirit is beautiful and complex beyond anything we can imagine.

If only more people understood just how powerful and loving that beautiful light is, maybe there wouldn't be as much suffering in this world. We suffer because we think we are alone. We suffer because we think we aren't enough. But nothing could be further from the truth.

Its past time that we realize how valuable we are to the light that holds us all together. We are so much a part of it all that even after our physical death, our spirit keeps on living, loving, learning, and even teaching.

Be still. Listen. Feel.

The light has been there all along.

Just reach for it.

—CHAPTER 16—
THE GUARDIAN SPIRIT

*A**westruck.*

This was how our next spirit visitor left me feeling. I was *so* in awe, in fact, that I could hardly breathe and only managed to get out a couple words when I spoke to it.

A few days earlier, I'd received a book in the mail about spirit guides. When I'd carried it upstairs, I'd discovered a white feather on my vest. I made note of it but didn't understand what it meant at the time or what it had to do with spirit guides.

A couple chapters into the book, though, I started to wonder. The book wasn't just on spirit guides; it was also about angels and archangels.

As I've mentioned in a couple chapters, I'm not comfortable using Christian names for spirits because of what I've experienced in my life, so along my spiritual awakening path, I started referring to angels as guardians because, well, that's what they do. They protect and serve The Great Spirit by keeping you safe and out of trouble.

Also, despite what you might think, I'm logical and a hound dog about debunking mysteries. I'm open-minded about a lot of subjects, but I don't take on any theories or beliefs unless I've seen them for myself. That's just how I work.

This being said, I definitely believe in and had encountered guardians (angels) before but didn't realize there was more to them than that.

The book was interesting, and I went in with an open mind. The author wrote that we are continually surrounded by a group of loving spirits who are sent here by God to guide you, help you, teach you, and even shower you in gifts, if you are open to them.

I read the chapters about archangels and immediately renamed them in my mind as "Elite Guardians". The author mentioned seven of them in her book and told a bit about them – their names, their purposes, and their personal energy.

She said that their main purpose is to serve The Creator, and that by caring for you and your needs, they serve The Creator. She said that we are *meant to call on them* because that is their purpose.

She said that archangels have a much bigger, more complicated job than regular angels because they are essentially The Great Spirit's hands. They motivate, inspire, challenge, protect, and shake things up in a good way. They are powerful, determined, and *get things done.*

She said if you ask them for help, you'd better be sure you want it because they *make things happen.*

For fun, I printed the Elite Guardians' names on a cool piece of photo paper, set it down, and headed off to bed.

The lights were off, and Kiani and I were both snuggled under the covers, ready to drift off.

It is my habit at bedtime to pray in my mind. It's usually directed at The Great Spirit, thanking him for his love and protection.

On this night, though, I didn't stop after I spoke to him. I paused and then said something like this inside my head:

Hey, uh...I would like to speak to The Elite Guardian or archangel known as Michael. Michael? If you can hear me, I just wanted to say 'hello'. I know I haven't spoken to you before, and

I'm not sure if you're much familiar with me, but I wanted to reach out, say 'hi', and introduce myself. I'm Sam.

Not even one second after I thought that, I felt a powerful presence standing over me on my side of the bed.

I *knew* instantly who and what it was, since I had encountered a guardian before, but *this one* was like a guardian times five hundred in the powerful presence department.

I gasped and turned my face and body toward it. I couldn't see it, but I *felt* it. It was immensely tall! It almost reached the ceiling, and its emotional energy was pure *love, joy, and affection.*

"Kiani!" I breathed, reaching my left arm behind me toward my daughter. "Do you see it?"

"Yes!" came the fast reply behind me. "What *is* that? There's white light everywhere!"

"It's Michael," I said softly. "The Elite Guardian."

I reached my hand out to where Michael stood and managed to get out three words:

Hi! and *Thank you!*

The beautiful being stood there for another handful of seconds, then gently vanished, leaving the air around him charged with energy.

As you can imagine, Kiani and I couldn't sleep for another couple hours after this. She wanted to know all about the Elite Guardians – their names, their personalities, and what their jobs were. She described Michael as being so bright that she could only make out two details: he was as tall as the ceiling and wore a white robe.

When we finally did fall asleep, it was the easiest and most comforting slumber we've ever had, as if we'd drifted off while wrapped up in all that was good and warm in the world.

—CHAPTER 17—
THE GHOST SNAKE

"Ghost snake?" you might ask.

To which I'd reply with, "Yep! They exist!"

My daughter and I are plenty used to animal spirits in our home – mostly cats and a few dogs. But even though we do have pet snakes, whom we love, it never once crossed our minds that there might be snake spirits.

Well, one day, Kiani started seeing what we thought was the residual energy of one of my pet ball pythons.

Residual energy is energy left behind by animal or human spirits. It can be solid, misty, or invisible and has no intelligence or awareness. It is much like an impression left behind, as if from a footstep in the carpet.

Kiani sometimes sees the residual energy of my

mother and me. She said we look like we always do and often do things we do a lot of, such as standing in the bathroom or sitting at a desk. Once, she said she saw me in the bathroom, putting make-up on, and watched me for a few seconds before turning around and heading into the bedroom, where she was startled to see me sitting on my sofa.

"Whoa! Mommy! How long have you been here?"

"Probably a half-hour. Why?"

"Because I just saw you in the bathroom!"

One day, she started seeing the misty form of a snake inside one of my ball python's tanks. She commented on it a few times, but again, we didn't put much thought into it.

Then, a week later, I started hearing sounds coming from the tank. I'm familiar with these sounds, as they are the typical gentle thumps that a pet snake makes when they move around a lot. My snakes love to reach up and sniff at the smells coming from the wire lid, and they often lose their balance and thump back down onto the ground.

They also make little *puff* sounds when they're trying to get your attention in some way, or when they get a bit of floor bedding stuck on their nose. I think they're adorable, honestly, but you'd have to be familiar with and appreciate pet snakes to relate.

The noises kept on, but when I would look at the tanks, every snake was always fast asleep.

(Many pet snakes, especially ball pythons, are lazy animals and spend a lot of their time sleeping or simply watching their favorite humans (one of mine even watches TV with me!) After twenty-five years of having snakes in my home, I got used to what a completely relaxed and possibly sleeping snake looks like.)

Again, I kept dismissing these noises as possible residual energy. I also knew that my clairaudience (psychic hearing) was improving, so I thought that had something to do with it as well.

Then, one night, Kiani was off at her friend's house when I distinctly heard a loud hiss and a *thunk*. It was unmistakably the sound of a stressed snake hitting the glass. My snakes are all calm, gentle creatures, who've never struck at anything other than the frozen/thawed mice I give them for their meals, so I was instantly alert and concerned.

But again, when I looked, *all my snakes* were sleeping peacefully.

What in the world is going on? I wondered. I

honestly didn't get it.

After that night, the sounds became even more frequent, and Kiani kept seeing that misty snake form in my female's tank.

To top this off, my poor python stopped eating and started moving around her tank almost constantly. She would only stop for short naps, then go right back to tank surfing. No matter how much I tried, she wouldn't calm down and refused all food I offered her.

I was beginning to get worried.

Then, a night or so later, Kiani saw the misty snake yet again, and it finally hit me.

My poor, stressed-out female must be reacting to the spirit of another snake in her tank. There couldn't be any other explanation.

I asked Kiani for help. We lit a bundle of sage, blew it out, and stood in front of the tank.

"Throw white light at it," I told her.

"Already on it," came her reply.

I spoke a few words.

"Snake spirit, we know you're here. This is not your home. You don't belong here, and you need to move on. We send you into the light. Leave now. Go on. Shoo!"

I blew sage smoke at the tank and even stood over it and gently blew some into the tank itself. Then I grabbed two black tourmaline stones and placed them inside the tank.

The effect was instant. The sounds stopped, the mist form vanished, and my female snake stopped moving. She stared curiously at us for a few moments, then curled into a corner and fell asleep.

My poor, little snake friend. I felt so bad for not helping her sooner. She wound up sleeping the whole night through, then slept all the next day. She woke up only briefly the following night to check if we were around, then went right back to sleep again.

Two days later, she was back to her normal, calm self and starting to show an interest in food again.

I still feel bad for not handling it sooner, but we definitely learned a few things from this experience:

1. Yes, all animals sense the spirit world.

2. Spirits come in all human and animal forms.

3. All of them can be sent out of your house, if needed.

—CHAPTER 18—
THE CHEERFUL SOLDIER

Things got rather intense for a couple months.

A spirit medium lady, whom I hadn't seen in a year, had been over to visit a few times. I will call her "Eve".

One night, when Eve was at my house, we decided to watch one of our favorite movies. My TV is in my bedroom. We were seated on a sofa along one wall, while Kiani was curled up on the bed, playing with her tablet.

We were halfway through the movie when the ceiling light started to flicker and then switched on. We both looked at the light in surprise, then at each other.

Eve's eyes turned in the direction of the doorway.

"Someone is here with us," she said.

I stood up and grabbed my spirit box and Ovilus, and she asked me if I had something she could use as a pendulum. I handed her an opalite necklace of mine, then sat back down, while she stood near the doorway.

My cats, who had been laying on my bed, jumped down and walked to me, then sat at my feet. I found this interesting.

"*Albert*," the spirit box said. We made note of this and then I turned it off, so we could concentrate without the static of the spirit box.

Eve held one hand out, palm-up, and held the pendulum over it.

"If there is someone here who'd like to speak with us, we are here to listen," Eve said. "You can move this pendulum for us," she continued. "Circle for yes, back and forth for no. Is there someone here?"

Yes.

"Were you the one who turned on the light?"

Yes.

"Are you a guide?"

No.

"Are you here because you like this house?"

Yes.

"Do you feel safe here?"

Yes.

"Are you here a lot?"

No.

"Are you just passing through?"

Yes.

"Did you turn on the light to get our attention?"

Yes.

"I get this feeling he is an older spirit," she told me. "Possibly from the Revolutionary War. His energy is playful. He has a good sense of humor and an infectious grin. I keep seeing these long socks in my head."

I grinned at this, as I was familiar with colonial clothing.

"Is this Weston?" I asked.

No.

"*British. Slain,*" said the Ovilus.

"Were you alive during the Revolutionary War? When the Americans fought the British?"

Yes.

"Were you a soldier?"

Yes.

"Is your name Albert?"

Yes.

"He won't come into the room. I wonder why," Eve said.

"Why won't you come into the room? Does the incense burning bother you?" we asked him.

No.

Eve's eyes lit up. "Oh, I know!" She addressed the spirit again. "The reason you won't come into this room... is it because it's improper to enter a woman's bedroom?"

Yes.

This made sense, as cultural etiquette was different in the 1700s than it is now.

"Let's try walking out to the living room and kitchen," Eve said.

I handed Eve my K2 meter (EMF detector), and Kiani and I followed. I left the Ovilus behind and took my phone along, which has an application on it meant for spirit communication.

(A lot of ghost hunters might scoff at using a phone app, but I've had accurate responses to situations and encounters using one. This, in my opinion, is because spirits are made of energy, which has been proven to affect electronics. In fact, two of my spirit guides (whom I finally made contact and conversed with) both use my phone to get my attention or to "talk" with me. One has been pulling my attention to my phone for four years at precise times having to do with elevens (a female teacher guide) and the other (a male protective guide; the cowboy) has been pulling my attention to forty-fours since the day Weston dropped a penny on Kiani's head. They also communicate strongly with me while using my tarot app. A skeptic observing this would be speechless.)

As Kiani and I stepped out into the living room and toward the kitchen, the spirit app said, "*Dinner serving.*"

I couldn't help laughing at this as I instantly got the joke from Albert. *That's quite the table over there. When are you serving dinner?* (My table *is* rather unusual-looking, but I love it.)

We moved around the room a bit more but got nothing on the K2 meter.

"He's not here anymore," said Eve. "I feel like he's gone downstairs to explore. He'll be back. Also," she added, "he's a little mischievous, this guy. He loves to laugh, and don't be surprised if some things go missing and turn back up quickly. That would be something he would find amusing."

I laughed. "Gotcha," I replied. Then, "Well, want

to finish that movie?"

"Absolutely!"

We didn't hear any more from him the rest of the night, but I have no doubt that he stuck around for a couple days.

Being an empath, I have a way of soaking up emotions around me. For two days after this incident, I found myself in a silly, goofy mood, always cracking smartass jokes at anyone around me. It was not unusual for me, but unusual to be that way consistently for two days.

Thanks for that, Albert! We all need a reminder to not take things so seriously.

—CHAPTER 19—
ALICE'S TEARS

Around this time, I was fortunate enough to be introduced to two of my spirit guides.

Since then, my connection with the spirit world and "spirit" (meaning The White Light, The Great Spirit, God, spirit guides, and guardians) has strengthened.

What I experienced at this point felt overwhelming at times, but I did my best to keep up. I feel like I will never stop learning – and not just in this lifetime either.

Before I tell you about what happened next, and without going into too much unnecessary details, I would like to quickly introduce my guides, which I'm sure you'll be hearing about from time to time. They are fast, strong communicators and help me understand a lot that confuses me.

Arthur

Arthur is a Guide to both my daughter and myself. He first made his presence known in Chapter 7. I didn't know who he was at the time, though. My daughter has seen him a few times and says he's dressed in jeans, boots, a vest, and a cowboy hat. He is a protective, grounding, strengthening guide with a good sense of humor and a kind heart – sort of grandfatherly. His spirit animal is the bee, and he's been using this cute little insect to send me messages for years. He even sends grumpy bees after people in my life whom he doesn't like.

Yona

Yona is a Cherokee woman who came into my life eighteen years ago, around the time I had the vision about the earthquake. She came to be my Teacher Guide and has been with me every step of the way on my spiritual journey. She is incredibly kind, sweet, and patient. Yona's spirit animal is the butterfly. It appears in various forms, highlighting spiritual path moments. Yona doesn't answer as many of my questions as Arthur does, but when she does, it's fast and powerful. She tries to get me to stop and *just feel* because half of the time, I know the answer inside of me already.

Now, back to the story.

Kiani and I were sitting on my bed, playing on our phones, when my TV, which sits across the room, suddenly logged out of Netflix and into my mother's YouTube channel (I don't know the password, nor have I ever logged onto her account).

Kiani and I looked at each other in surprise then turned our heads back to the TV. It wasn't done, either. From YouTube, it then started playing a video on health and wellness, then switched after a few seconds to a video playing Christian gospel music.

Kiani and I jumped up and walked over to the TV.

"What in the world?" I said. I was dumbfounded.

"How is that even possible?" Kiani asked me.

"I have no idea. The remote is sitting right there too," I told her, gesturing at the coffee table. "No one has touched it. Quick," I said, "run downstairs and see what's on Grandma's TV. Maybe hers is affecting ours somehow."

Kiani took off downstairs, and the TV paused itself before she reached the ground floor.

I stared, open-mouthed, at it for a couple seconds, then walked to the top of the stairs.

Kiani's voice sounded from below. "IT'S NOT ON!" she shouted.

"ARE YOU SERIOUS?" I shouted back.

I headed partway down the stairs and peered over the railing at my mom's black TV screen, then at my mom, who sat quietly reading a book in her favorite living room chair.

Kiani came back up and sat on the bed, and I grabbed my Ovilus.

At this point, I had no doubt the TV had been manipulated by a spirit, so I decided to try talking to it.

I turned the Ovilus on and set it on the coffee table in front of the TV. "Hello, spirit," I said. "I know you don't mean any harm. You're welcome to rest here a while, if you like."

Instantly, the Ovilus piped up with, "Thanks."

"Wow! You're welcome," I replied. "I *would* like to request that you stop messing with my TV, though," I added. "It's a little freaky."

In quick response to this, the TV went black.

I tried using my tarot cards to get more information from her but couldn't, partly because I tried using a different method than my usual.

A name did come up on the Ovilus, though.

Alice.

I made note of it and couldn't help but notice that this was probably around the eighth time that name had appeared on the device since I'd gotten it a few months before.

The next night, while Kiani was visiting her dad, I had a couple friends over to play card games. One was Eve, the spirit medium, and the other was a guy named Gus. He's a kind, gentle soul who loves to laugh and talk deeply on a variety of subjects.

We had just finished dinner and were talking at my kitchen table when Eve turned her head toward the living room and said, "I feel like someone is here."

Then, later, "Wow, they are not going away, either. Whoever it is *really* wants to talk."

I set about turning on a couple of my spirit communication devices, and Eve tried talking to the spirit using a couple different decks of cards before requesting her go-to method, the pendulum. I quickly fetched one for her.

Eve then held one hand out, palm-up, with the pendulum above it, held in the other hand.

"Okay, let's try this," she said. "If there is a spirit here who would like to talk to us, you can use this. Make it move in a circle for yes and back and forth for no. Is there a spirit here?"

Yes.

"Do you need help?"

YES!

"Were you the spirit who used my TV last night?" I asked.

Yes.

"Is your name Alice?"

YES.

I remembered the gospel music the spirit put on the TV.

"Are you a Christian?"

Yes.

Eve took a deep breath and steadied the pendulum. "Wow, she is so anxious!" Then, to the spirit, "Easy. Slow down. We're here. We're listening."

Throughout all this, my K2 meter (EMF detector), which sat on the end of the table, near

Eve, kept spiking up into the red zone.

Eve continued.

"What bought you here?" She paused, then said, "She's showing me her church group."

(We initially thought Alice was a friend of my mom's from California, who had passed away three days prior. Afterward, having connected a few dots and spoken to my guides, we knew it wasn't her. This Alice had been around my home for months, trying to get help.)

"Is there something we can do for you?" Eve asked.

YES!

"I feel like it's a man...husband...is it your husband?"

YES!

"She wants us to get a message to her husband," Eve said.

At this point, the most incredible and bizarre thing happened me. Being an empath, it makes perfect sense now, but it shocked me at the time.

I *felt* Alice's tremendous relief at finally being heard and understood. It shot through my heart like an arrow, and I started sobbing.

"This isn't me!" I managed to get out before my

hands covered my face. I gave into the sensation and just sobbed for a little while. Then, just as suddenly as it hit me, it pulled back and vanished.

"We don't know who her husband is. How are we supposed to help her?" I asked.

Eve and Gus could only shake their heads sadly.

A moment of inspiration hit me.

"How about we pray for you and your husband, Alice? Would that work?"

YES!

I looked at Eve and Gus. They nodded encouragingly.

(Eve told me later that when I started praying, she felt Alice reach out and take hold of her hand. She said she will never forget that feeling.)

"Dear Heavenly Father," I began, "Alice is here with us, and she's suffering. She is worried about her husband. I ask that you be with her. Put your hands on her, and send her guardian angel to be by her side. And Father, please send her husband's guardian angel to be with him. Comfort him, and help him to know how much Alice loves him. Help him through the loss of his wife. I also ask that when Alice is ready, that you send her angel to gently wrap his wings around her and guide her into the light, where she can be with you in Heaven. All this, I ask in Jesus' name. Amen."

I barely got out the last sentence because *again,* the emotional arrow hit me, and I cried harder this time. I cried Alice's tears of tremendous gratitude and relief.

I can go now. Oh, thank you! I felt her say.

Then she pulled back and was gone.

At this point, my spirit guide, Arthur, who had accompanied Yona to be with us during the session, made the K2 meter light up. His voice, edged in humor, broke the silence in Eve's head.

"He wants to know if we're playing cards or just going to sit here."

—CHAPTER 20—
GHOSTS LIKE PUPPIES TOO

I'm used to my cats and even my pet ball python seeing and reacting to our ghostly visitors, but up until this point, our new puppy hadn't shown any signs of seeing anything.

I will call him "Muppet" in this book, mainly because he looks like one to me sometimes. I've been told that he's so cute that he doesn't look real, like he should be a cartoon character. I'd have to agree, so Muppet works.

One night, I was sitting on my sofa in my bedroom, watching a cute paranormal show about two psychic mediums from the U.K. who take house calls to help confused or pesky spirits into the light.

I admit to being rather charmed by these ladies' personalities. They are good at what they do but also have great humor, love to laugh, and have an adorable habit of grabbing onto each other and yelping when something startles them. I couldn't stop at just one episode, so I'd settled in to binge-watch with a cup of tea.

A few minutes into the show, I started getting goosebumps. This isn't unusual, and though, sometimes, it can mean the presence of a spirit, most of the time, I think nothing of it. If it's coming from me – meaning a reaction to something emotionally touching – I usually know because I feel either excited or moved when it happens.

Three episodes into the show, though, I started to wonder what was going on. I was getting goosebumps every five minutes or so, and I didn't feel like it matched what I was feeling while watching the program. A couple instances, I felt genuinely touched by what the ladies were doing, but I wasn't feeling much of anything the rest of the time.

At one point, I said to my daughter, "Man, there must be some spirit here with us who is really into this show. I never get goosebumps this much."

Kiani looked up and watched me for a moment but didn't see anything at first.

A few minutes later, she came and sat next to

me. Muppet soon followed and then started wiggling his way between our legs on the floor.

Kiani suddenly gasped.

"Whoa! Mommy!" she said, "I just saw a hand and arm reach out and start petting Muppet!"

"Really?" I said, looking down at the wiggling puppy. I didn't see anything, of course. This was my daughter's specialty.

"Yeah! It had this rainbow-colored energy around it too! It was cool!"

I paused the show, turned on my spirit-sensing devices, and grabbed my tarot deck.

The Ovilus quickly piped up with the words, "BIG MATTER RELIGION JUDGE SOUL ALONE CONTRITION."

"Goodness! Slow down!" I exclaimed.

I pulled a few cards from my tarot deck and got the sense that there was more than one spirit. At least one of them felt guilty about the life they'd led and worried about going into the light.

I tried to explain that they had nothing to fear from the light and that there were loved ones waiting for them there. I told them that we were going to attempt to make a doorway for them. I couldn't force them to go but assured them it would be okay if they did. I also said that if we failed to make a doorway, or if they changed their mind later, they could always seek out a funeral home and follow one of the many departing souls walking through the light.

I asked Kiani for help, and together, we visualized a doorway to the light on a wall to our left.

"What's that?" the spirit box said.

"Appearance," said the Ghost Radar. Then, "Stay."

"A white orb just flew out of the wall!" Kiani exclaimed, pointing at the area we were focusing on. "I also heard a child's voice say something I couldn't understand."

We held the visualization of the door for a few moments longer, then let it go.

I'm honestly not sure if any of the spirits went through, but there was a change of energy after that. I kept watching the show for another couple episodes, but the goosebumps never returned.

I'm glad that one of the spirits found Muppet irresistible, or we might not have thought to make contact.

Muppet wasn't quite done attracting spirits after

this, either.

The next morning, I came upstairs after a bath to the sight of Kiani, wide-eyed and gesturing for me to come closer.

She said that while I'd been downstairs, Muppet had reacted to an invisible someone entering the bedroom.

She said he had been contentedly chewing on his bone when he suddenly looked at the doorway, dropped the bone, and then ran toward someone unseen. He was excitedly wagging his tail, licking his lips, and straining his head up in the direction of something standing above him.

"Well, I'll be damned," I said, staring wonderingly at Muppet. "So much for him not seeing ghosts."

—CHAPTER 21—
ENERGY CORDS

I feel like I learned a lot around this time. I expected more of the same in the new year, in regard to spirit activity (only the occasional ghost sighting or sounds and never any low-level ones), but that was not what we got. I do understand that our house has a comforting light about it, which can be restful for some spirits, but by mid-March, the number of spirits in my house had grown so much that it was becoming a little confusing.

Why so much? What had changed?

And to top off the increase in gentle spirits, we also started having problems with low-level spirits, which we hadn't encountered in over a year and a half. They couldn't get *in* the house, but they certainly tried.

All I knew to do was to just keep praying about it

and talking to The Great Spirit and trust that it was happening for a reason.

By the end of March, things had gone completely back to normal.

Why? It took me a couple days to connect the dots, but I finally figured it out.

When you think of hauntings, you think of houses, right? Well, people can be haunted as well (by both humans and spirits). There are invisible cords of energy that connect us to other people whom we've shared intense emotion with – and not just people we've met either.

Sometimes, cords can form from a heated or emotional conversation between two people online. Think back on your own online experiences. Have you ever been involved in some sort of a dignified debate with someone, and they suddenly turned vicious and lashed out at you? How did you feel afterward? Did you sleep well? Did it leave you with a disturbed kind of feeling? Did you keep thinking about it?

I think if people aren't careful to avoid angry people and drama in general, then one can become quickly "strung up" with cords of energy. They are all connected to you and your vitality, therefore affecting your energy levels, your peace of mind, your health, and even the health and peace of mind of the people closest to you, who are likewise connected to *you*. That's quite a tangle of cords, isn't it?

I believe an unexpected effect of these cord connections is that they can also act as spirit pathways between people. If that guy at work who yelled at you and called you names has a grumpy spirit of an old man attached to him, what's stopping that spirit sucking energy off *your* energy cord, which is now throwing out delicious hurt as the result of the name-calling? Your cord is now attached to his favorite human, after all. Fair game!

Cords or spirit attachments between spirits and humans can be the most harmful of them all. Psychics, spirit mediums, and people suffering greatly from mental illness can be especially vulnerable to spirit attachments, if they are not careful to keep a strong and steady connection to The Light (the source of love), both within their homes and within themselves.

We can't always stop these cords from forming (though I have discovered that wearing black tourmaline or black obsidian can stop most negative ones), and some of them are beneficial, like the ones to your children and loving family members. Ever wonder why you feel so connected sometimes? How they call you right when you think of them?

But we can start by being aware of the cords. Once you are, then the next logical step would be careful consideration when it comes to who we choose to bring into our lives and how we choose to connect with strangers, family, clients, coworkers, etc. Keep your vibes up! Choose your words carefully, and let nothing come from your mouth that does not come from love.

Every negative word from you and every negative action has a dark reaction. It fills your spirit with darkness and pushes out the light, which is our only true protection.

Emotions, thoughts, and intentions are powerful. You can cut a toxic person out of your life or drive a spirit entity off your property and into the setting sun, but if your energy is especially appealing to a negative person or an entity, the cord can sometimes stay attached. It can affect your sense of peace, your mood, and your focus.

How do you cut them? Here's how I do it.

(Depending on how strong you feel the cord is, you can start with an Epson salt bath first, then...) Sit by yourself somewhere, close your eyes, and visualize the sky above you opening up and spilling down intense, love-filled, white light. See yourself completely covered in it. Take deep breaths and breathe in the white light.

Next, visualize each positive loved one's cord attached to you and gently set them aside to your left or right. Then take a piece of selenite or just your hand and visualize holding a flaming, hot, white and blue sword or knife. Visualize and even mime cutting around your body, leaving your loved ones' cords untouched at your side. See in your mind the unwanted cords snapping, breaking, and shriveling off from your body, like burning hair or rope fibers. Pay the most care at the front of your body, near the stomach, and your back.

Once that is done, smudge your body the best you can with some dried sage to finish and then you're done! You will feel it too! A wonderful sense of lightness and peace.

—CHAPTER 22—
GHOST MOUSE

We have quite the little zoo at our house. Dog, cats, hamsters, fish, a rabbit, pet snakes, and pet mice. It's a whole house *brimming with adorable*. I love it.

I feel like animals are on a closer frequency to The Great Spirit than humans are. I look into their loving, open little faces, and I see The Creator. It fills me with a sense of love and gratitude.

February and March were rough months for us with our pets, though. We had a group of female mice who had been with us for two and a half years and one by one, we started losing them to the ravages of time. I hadn't cried that much since the move here. I love pocket pets, but their lives are so heartbreakingly short compared to their intelligence and affectionate ways.

We were down to only two of the original girls and then, one day, I saw the light starting to go out of the eyes of our favorite: an adorably chubby little mouse named Frances.

We spoiled her rotten the last few days with us. Even though she didn't feel well, she never once turned down a treat, such was her love of food. When she passed, I buried her in the front yard, close to her other mouse friends, who'd gone before her.

A week went by and then, one night, Kiani happened to glance at the mouse tank on her way to the kitchen for a snack. Frances was there, chubby as ever, running happily away on a little mouse wheel. Kiani said she didn't think anything of it at first and looked away but then stopped in her tracks when she realized what she'd seen. She turned back, but Frances was gone. There was only an empty, still moving wheel, which came to a slow stop as she stood there watching, no mouse in sight.

This was the first sighting of a spirit mouse in our home, which is surprising considering that we've had quite a few mice. When you think about it, though, it made sense. With Frances gone, Minnie would now be by herself. Frances must have decided that instead of leaving Minnie, she'd stick around for a while longer. Besides...Minnie couldn't possibly handle all those delicious treats on her own, right? That's what friends are for.

—CHAPTER 23—
HITCHHIKING GHOSTS

My mom came back from a trip to Los Angeles one day with the spirit of a little boy in tow.

My mom has what I call "The Pied Piper Gene". It is half of what my grandfather had, and she has it *strong!* (I, in turn, have half of hers). Kids are drawn to her like moths to a flame. When we are out in public, children stare in fascinated wonder at my mother, as if she were a combination of a movie princess, a knight in full armor, and a giant chocolate chip cookie. When my mom looks back, they smile from ear to ear. Kids wave at her, babies reach for her, and parents often have to drag them away while they stare back at my mom, slack-jawed. I've seen it countless times, and it never ceases to amaze me.

I also know that busy, public places are *packed*

with spirits. The more chaotic, busy, or tense the human energy, the more the ghosts there are soaking it up, like a pack of sunbathing teenage girls. And if these ghosts see someone they find especially fascinating – either someone they relate to or whose energy feels especially soothing – they will sometimes follow that person home.

There is no doubt in my mind one of them hitchhiked home with my mom this time.

It had been quiet prior to this. I'd cut a few energy cords to some negative people in my life, cleansed and sealed the house again, and was enjoying the immediate benefits.

The first night after her return wasn't too eventful, other than an owl hooting repeatedly outside my bedroom window (owls mean big change and that you are being guided and protected on your spiritual journey).

But the following day felt weird. Kiani kept seeing flashes of copper light, and my ears kept ringing while I was interacting with my daughter or the animals (ear-ringing can sometimes be your body's way of picking up on spirits; it is common in some sensitive people and not always a result of ear damage). Then Kiani saw a little boy briefly appear at the top of the stairs.

Following this, Kiani and I had what I can only call "bothered dreams". For hours, they went on, and the last one kind of freaked me out, to be honest. In it, a little boy leaned over me while I slept and talked and talked and talked. I couldn't make out what he was saying, but when he started to pull on my blanket over my shoulder, I startled awake.

I admit to not handling it as gently as I could have, and I feel bad, but no one likes to be bugged while sleeping. I sat up and chewed the boy out, like a frustrated parent would.

"Out!" I said. "Get out. Now!"

Kiani woke up and asked what was happening. I sighed and explained briefly, then we both fell asleep again, this time with no spirit or dream interruptions.

The following day was a lot calmer. No ear-ringing, except when my Mom cut up a giant lemon meringue pie and sat down with the kids to eat it. When I walked over to join them, back the ringing came. I wish I could have offered the kid a piece of pie for yelling at him, but I decided I would have to settle for having a talk with him next time we sensed him.

—CHAPTER 24—
HOW *GHOSTS LIKE BACON* GOT ITS NAME AND OTHER STORIES

When I first started writing about our ghostly adventures, I was trying to think of what to call it. I wanted something cute and not scary because I feel like my whole purpose is to banish fear, not to welcome it.

For some reason, I kept thinking back on this one occasion, when I first got my spirit box and was getting to know how it worked. In a burst of silliness, I started talking about food to see if I could get any responses and wound up getting quite a few of them. They went something like this: "Bacon, coffee, latte, bacon, cream, ketchup, bacon." From this, I concluded that *ghosts must really like bacon!*

It kind of sucks that the spirit box is so loud and

staticky between voices, though. I don't use it much because of that. Since I'm on the subject, though, I thought I'd share another spirit box incident that was *amazing!* One day, inspired by another of my silly moods, I decided to turn the box on when I felt that *room full of unusual energy* feeling I often get when spirits are close.

I grabbed a pencil next to me, and I asked if anyone in the room knew what the object was called.

"Pencil," a man's voice said.

Wow!

Curious, I set the pencil down and picked up a few other objects. One by one, the names popped up over the box. "Pipe, cup, crystal."

(I still have this recording and will probably share it to the public at some point.)

Another interesting incident happened back when the house was rather fuller of ghosts than usual – especially children. I was sitting on my bed when I felt an area of my arm go warm, as if from a small hand, but without the weight of it. I don't remember ever feeling a sensation quite like that. To make sure it wasn't just some random thing my body was doing, I reached my hand out next to me and said, "Can you touch me again please? Can you take my hand?"

Instantly, I felt the same warm sensation on my hand. Again, the area was small, like a young child's hand would be.

And speaking of children! We were finally able to help the little boy who followed my mom home.

He stopped going in my room for a while after I got grumpy at him for waking me up, but that little guy *loved sweets!* Every time one of us was eating a cookie, a piece of pie, or ice cream bar, I would get this gentle little ring in my right ear, always the same pitch and tone (I'm beginning to catch on that each spirit has its own ringtone, so to speak).

The last time this happened, Kiani came bounding into my bedroom with a little mochi ice cream ball in her hand. She climbed over to her favorite corner of my bed to enjoy it, and *here came that same gentle ringing* in my right ear.

I seized the opportunity and tried talking to him. I told him I was sorry for being cross at him when he woke me up, and I talked to him about his family and what would be waiting for him in the light, if he was ready to go. I felt I might have been especially convincing with my talk of "all the sweets you can eat" on the other side (and I truly believe this!).

After my little speech, I turned my ghost phone app on (just in case I could catch any words) and then I closed my eyes and envisioned a doorway of light.

Out loud, I said, "Great Spirit, please be with me as I work to create this doorway. I ask that my Guardian Spirit be here to help, as well as The Elite Guardian, Michael. And I would like to ask for my spirit guides' help in communicating. Please be my eyes and my ears. I would like to call forth any family members of the little boy or any family members of the other spirits in this room. Please step forward and help these spirits to cross over to you."

One second after I finished saying this, my ear rang at a high pitch, goosebumps rose on my arms, and the ghost radar popped up with "AID."

Then followed a flurry of energy that lasted for maybe thirty seconds and all went still.

We never saw or felt him again after that.

—CHAPTER 25—
OUT OF THE DARKNESS

At this point, almost two years had passed since Kiani came to me about her ability to see spirits. I couldn't help but be amazed at the changes in our lives.

Before, both of us suffered almost every night with nightmares and night terrors (for me, they had been lifelong; I didn't know what a good night's sleep was). I also suffered from random bouts of depression and exhaustion, which sometimes left me almost unable to function.

My daughter's anxiety was bad. She was so scared of going anywhere without me that even playdates and birthday parties were a challenge.

The type of spirits my daughter saw regularly were frightening. Red-eyed creatures staring at her through windows, ghosts with sunken eyes and missing body parts, reptilian creatures, floating human torsos, black shapes lurking in corners of our house and on the sidewalk below, black orbs streaking past her face, black arms and hands reaching out of walls and floors, and menacing laughter coming from nowhere. It was truly no wonder my daughter felt terrified. This is no way for anyone to live, let alone a child.

Kiani also suffered with a constant sense of being "bombarded" with energy that wasn't hers. Not knowing why or what was happening to her, her mind and spirit instinctively responded to this by throwing out her own energy in the form of constant movement, constant chatter, and random silly noises. Kiani was *never* quiet or still. Even when she slept, it never stopped. She would thrash, whimper, and grind her teeth almost every night. She had trouble focusing on schoolwork, and even though she loved to draw, she couldn't do it for long.

Now, after learning spiritual protection, nightmares and night terrors are in the past for us. We sleep peacefully. Kiani's thrashing, whimpering, and teeth grinding have stopped. My unexplainable bouts of depression and exhaustion have stopped.

Kiani can now sit quiet and still for hours. The need for constant movement and noise has been greatly reduced. Her drawing skills and schoolwork have improved, along with her focus in general.

Kiani's need to be constantly with me has changed as well. She loves going to slumber parties and parks with her friends, can sleep on her own if she needs to, and loves to walk down the street to the neighbor kids' houses.

The scary sounds, dark shapes, and disturbing ghosts are gone and with them, Kiani's fear of the spirit world. With that fear gone, she's been enjoying lots of new experiences.

For almost a year now, Kiani keeps seeing a little red light. It looks exactly like a laser light dot. It appears for a few seconds at a time on creative projects that she is working on (she loves to draw especially!), and once, it appeared on a little, framed photograph of one of my deceased grandfather's handwritten poems.

I wasn't sure what to make of it at first. Having now read accounts of spirit guides often appearing as tiny dots of light, I'm almost certain it's one of her guides. Time will tell.

Kiani also started developing a new ability a few

months ago. I've been told it's called "Clairaudience" and includes not only hearing the spirit world (which she was doing already) but hearing sounds that aren't physically within her range of hearing (a bit like when a psychic sees something in their head that is happening elsewhere).

On two occasions, she has heard snatches of conversation between two or more people, which took place anywhere from thirty to fifty feet outside the building while she was inside, with the windows and door closed. She said it sounded exactly like they were standing right next to her when they were definitely not.

She was a little spooked by it at first, but I think she's settled in with the idea for the most part.

I can't wait to see how her abilities develop over the years, and now, neither can Kiani.

She said the most wonderful thing to me one day.

"Mommy, is it weird that I think ghosts are boring now?"

I laughed. "No! It's not weird! It's awesome! Your abilities will always be there if you need them, but for now, you can just relax and be a regular kid."

"You know what I might do when I grow up, though?"

"What's that?" I asked, curious.

"Maybe I can be a psychic for the police and help them find missing people. Wouldn't that be COOL?"

"Ki, that would be AMAZING."

—CHAPTER 26—
GHOSTLY CONCLUSIONS

I'm going to end with a few of my conclusions on the spirit world.

Please keep in mind that I don't consider myself to be an expert on this subject. I'm simply a person whose experiences have piled up over the years, to the point where I'm comfortable stating my theories and thoughts on the subject, which, in my opinion, is only a drop of knowledge in one *large* bucket. One of my favorite sayings is, *"The only true knowledge is knowing that you know nothing."*

As with anything you read or hear, run this information past that place in your heart where your truth lives, and let it pass by if it doesn't resonate with you.

I guess the best way to do this is to answer my own previous questions.

Were ghosts once living beings?

I believe it's possible that *not all* of them were, but yes, I think the majority were once alive in physical form, whether it was as a human, animal, extraterrestrial, or even a plant.

Why are they here? Why not cross over into The Light?

The ones who don't cross over are called Earthbound spirits. I believe there are a few reasons that they stay:

1. They are scared to cross over for fear of getting in trouble. I think the majority of these spirits believe "Hell" awaits them in some form. If they don't believe in hell, they might simply be afraid of facing deceased loved ones who might be angry with them (this is silly, though, because spirits who cross over into the light no longer possess resentment, anger, etc.)

2. They don't want to leave their living loved ones. These spirits stay in hopes of watching over the people who meant so much to them. What they don't understand, though, is that they can't do

much of anything as an Earthbound spirit. If they're lucky, a sensitive, living human can sense them in some way, but I think even moving objects around takes a lot of effort and energy. These spirits would be in a much better position to help once they've crossed over. Not only can they come back to visit loved ones when needed, send animal messages, etc., but they can also interact with their loved ones in dreams, with full conversations. And what's even cooler than that is that sometimes, they might even be given the role of *Spirit Guide* to a loved one, which is the case with our Spirit Guide, Arthur.

3. They stay because they're simply curious. Once out of the body, they realize this is a new experience, and they want to see what they can do and where they can go. I imagine this is a snoopy person's wildest dream come true because they can watch people without anyone knowing. Lovely, huh?

4. Confusion. This one is the worst and saddest in my opinion. If you've ever heard the term "trapped spirit", this is the type I'm talking about. When a human dies while in a state of extreme anger, frustration, obsession, or fear, they can become trapped in these negative emotional

energies and sometimes not even be aware of where they are or who they are with. Some, in rare occasions, may not even be aware (or simply unable to accept) that they are dead.

I call this plane of existence "The Hell Realm". I don't personally believe in the Biblical Hell, but if it were to exist, this would be it.

I believe that a lot of spirits exist within this realm, many of which include former victims of drugs, violence, or any other terrible habit or obsession that can be hard to let go of.

I think they stay in this state of confusion until they suddenly "come to" and realize they've had enough and want to move on, or they are helped out of this state by another Earthbound spirit, a spirit who has crossed over, or by an experienced psychic medium working with Spirit Guides and Guardian Spirits.

What are low-level spirits?

I consider low-levels to be any spirit with negative or dark energy, like someone who died carrying a lot of anger, depression, or resentment. I think low-levels can be anything from a deeply depressed housewife to a former killer obsessed with violence. In fact, I think what people call demons are just *old* murderers and sociopaths who, having died, refused to pass into the light. Imagine how intelligent, powerful, and evil these beings could potentially become after thousands or millions of years wandering the earth?

What do spirits need to function?

Without the body, the human soul is just energy. It may not always be active, but it will always exist. For the Earthbound spirit to function, though, they need living, human energy. Many people think that spirits can pull energy from electronics, but I haven't found this to be true. I think they can easily affect electronics and do so often, but I highly doubt they get their energy from them.

Whatever energetic emotion the spirit gives out is also what they need in return. If they are an angry spirit, they will try to arouse that emotion in living humans to get the energy they need. If they were angry and dominant, fear is especially satisfying. If they were depressed, they look for and feed off humans who are feeling sad.

But what about the cheerful ghosts? There are quite a bit of these, as my daughter and I can attest to. These spirits get their energy from the higher frequency human emotions, such as excitement, joy, humor, and even love.

How do ghosts affect us?

As a lot of people are aware of or might suspect, the energy pulled from us by spirits affects our minds and bodies. We can feel drained or tired (and even develop chronic fatigue syndrome), we can develop a variety of health problems and illnesses (a lowering of the immune system in general) and, of course, our moods and even interests can be vastly affected by a spirit's presence as well.

What has been interesting to me, though, is that while the sad, angry spirits seem to affect us negatively, the cheerful ones don't have that affect. So far, my daughter and I have yet to feel drained or sick in their presence. To me, that says a lot about the power of positive thoughts and emotion.

What should I do about ghosts in my house?

Well, obviously, you don't want low-levels or even just the mildly grumpy ones in your home. And those can be kicked out quite easily using the techniques I mentioned in Chapter 6.

But what about the cheerful ones?

Truly and honestly, that's up to you and the ghost. If you don't mind them around, then let them be, but do try to remember that while they are Earthbound, their soul is on hold, so to speak. Whether you believe in reincarnation or just Heaven, these spirits can't move on with their destiny while wandering through your living room, being glared at by your house cat. They have loved ones waiting for them in The Light and things they could be accomplishing, which they cannot do here.

On the other hand, while you can tell them to leave (the kind ones will), you can't force them to cross over. Free Will is a Universal/Omniversal Law, and though you can tell them where to go to find The Light and even make it for them yourself, a spirit has to make that final decision themselves. In my opinion, most would cross over willingly if they understood things a little better.

Another of my favorite sayings is, *"The farthest distance between two people is misunderstanding."* I think this applies well here because having no understanding of what is *in* The Light, or how they will be greeted there, these spirits can't see *why* they should go.

Furthermore, if you were to go one step deeper into this thought process and believe that everything happens for a reason, then perhaps the ghost in your house was meant to find you... *so that they can finally make it back to their real home.*

Don't you think that's an amazing thought? I do.

—ABOUT THE AUTHOR—

Samantha Red Wolf started writing at age ten, but nothing felt right until she started *Ghosts Like Bacon*. She hopes that her stories will go a long way toward helping families like her own. Sam is currently studying for a career in alternative medicine, but in her free time, she enjoys reading, painting, playing the acoustic guitar, drinking craft beer, and being a big kid as much as she can get away with.

Samantha lives in North Carolina, USA with her two kids, her best friend (mom), and their many spoiled animal friends.

You can find her on Facebook at **facebook.com/samantha.redwolf.9**.

This book is always available to read in blog format at **www.ghostslikebacon.com**.

Made in the USA
Coppell, TX
22 March 2021